A Survival Guide For The Year 2000 Problem

Consumer Solutions For The Worst Technical Blunder In History

by

Jim Lord

ISBN 0-9660200-0-6

Dedication

To my family and to my shipmate,
Mike. With wealth such as this, what
does it matter if all the rest is lost?

Acknowledgements

I have sometimes heard sports announcers refer to the people in the stands at a football game as the "twelfth man." This happens when the crowd's high-energy level somehow succeeds in influencing the course of the game as if they were actually on the field with the team. I had such a crowd cheering me on in the writing of this book and the task could not have been done without them.

My wife, Betty the Sweet was first among these. There were countless days when I arrived home from work after dark, grabbed dinner and then disappeared into "the pit" (the basement where my office was located) until long after she had gone off to bed. Added to these were most weekends for over half a year as well as several periods of leave. Her hands were virtually on the keyboard with mine. Thanks hon.

My sons Ron the Exuberant (with his wife Jerri the Artistic), James the Searcher, Vail the Warrior (U.S.M.C.), Mason the Buddy and Gabe the Poet; my daughters Crystal the Focused and Becki the Fashionable and even my fine eldest grandson Ryan the Eagles Fan always made me feel like the stands were full.

I am also grateful for the encouragement I received from the folks at work. Frank Wooldridge, Kelly Brown, Chuck Droz and Nancy Korpela were first among these but many others were supportive as well. And a special thanks to Joe Fox who inspires us all.

Special thanks to my brother, Gary, who always had the courage to criticize. Also to Jack Price, the best printer in the world and to my exceptional editor, Ed Sapp.

Thanks a million, folks.

Table of Contents

Disclaimer

This publication has been written to provide the author's opinion regarding the subject matter discussed. It is sold with the understanding that the Author is not engaged in rendering legal, accounting or any other professional service. If legal, accounting or any other professional service is required, the services of a competent professional service provider should be sought.

The author specifically disclaims any personal liability, loss or risk incurred as a consequence of the use and application, either directly or indirectly, of any advice or information presented herein.

*"Dear Sir or Madam, will you read my book,
it took me years to write, will you take a look?"*

"Paperback Writer" - the Beatles

Chapter 1

Introduction

Just imagine ...

You can't believe what's happening. Your credit cards were all rejected at the grocery store but it didn't matter because there wasn't much food left in the store anyway. You need cash but the ATM machines are all shut down and every bank in town is closed. You're nearly out of gas but there are huge lines at every gas station. The stock market dropped over a thousand points today but you can't get in touch with your broker because the phones don't work either. There are National Guard troops at every corner and you can hear sirens all over town. There is smoke in the distance and that noise sounds like gunfire. Even the traffic lights are on the blink.

Has everyone gone crazy?

No - just the computers.

It's Y2K, the "Millennium Time Bomb."

Calamity?

This Survival Guide is about the worst technical problem the world has ever faced, commonly referred to as The Year 2000 Problem or "Y2K". At the very least, Y2K will cause serious disruptions across every aspect of our society. At the very worst, it will cause the greatest economic and social calamity the world has known since the Great Depression.

Defining The Y2K Problem

Y2K is short for "Year 2000." The letter "K" is an abbreviation for the Latin word "kilo" meaning one thousand. The Year 2000 Problem is simply this ...

> *Because of bad programming and poor technical management, computers will make date-related mistakes as we move into the new century. Fixing these computers is an extraordinarily large and complex task. Because we have waited so long to get started, it is no longer possible to fix them all.*

From the dawn of the computer age, shortcuts have been taken in the way computers use dates. We do the same thing ourselves by saying "ninety six" when we really mean "nineteen ninety six." As human beings, we can easily interpret this shorthand but computers won't be able to handle this lack of precision as we approach the Year 2000. The closer we get to the Year 2000, the more frequent and the more serious these errors will become.

Some computers will simply stop and refuse to function. Others will keep working but will give incorrect results. This doesn't sound too bad until you consider that the computer that stops might be the one that writes your paycheck. Or the one that doesn't work right makes a mistake in processing your mortgage payment. Or one of those really old computers at the IRS botches your income tax return. Many more very unpleasant examples will be provided in this Survival Guide.

Viral Infection

The Year 2000 Problem is sometimes referred to as "The Most Deadly Virus In History." Other names are the "Millennium Bug," or the "Doomsday Virus." In many ways, Y2K does behave like a virus. For example, bad data from one computer can "infect" another computer. A thousand computers could all get sick at once if they were hooked up in a network as many machines are today. It is even possible to "cure" a computer of its Y2K "disease" and have it "reinfected" again at a later date. This characteristic is one of the things that makes the Year 2000 Problem so difficult.

Computer Junkies

The fact is, we are completely dependent on computers and, in many ways, can't live without them. They are deeply involved in every aspect of our lives as I will demonstrate throughout this book. Millions of these computers around the world are going to get very, very sick, many of them all at once. As in any illness, no one knows for sure exactly how sick the patient is going to be. The experts do agree on one thing, however. The problem is unbelievably huge and incredibly complex.

Here are examples of some of the social, economic and personal difficulties that could be caused by Y2K.

- Erroneous termination or incorrect payment of

government benefits such as Social Security, welfare, food stamps and pensions

- Rampant medical malpractice as patients are refused, misdiagnosed or treated for the wrong condition

- The collapse of banks and insurance companies as
well as stock brokerages and exchanges

- Massive business failures as tens of thousands of
companies declare bankruptcy rather than take on
the costs of repairing their computer systems

- The contamination of legal information such as real
estate transaction records, driver's license data, tax
records and voter registration files

- Massive and persistent outages of electrical power,
water, sewage treatment and telephone service

- Widespread disruptions in emergency services such
as police, fire fighter and ambulance

- The most severe traffic jams ever seen

- Widespread riots and civil disturbances in the major
cities

- The accidental, wholesale release of dangerous prisoners from prisons and jails

Oh, and don't let me forget ...

- The **greatest explosion of lawsuits in history** !

Could This Really Be True?

Leading computer software experts now freely admit there is a grave problem. The government, the press, the business community and the academic world have finally gotten on the wagon with this issue. For a time, there were many who claimed Y2K was an artificial problem, a scare tactic cooked up by the information technology industry to create business for themselves. There are still some detractors but their numbers are dwindling rapidly as serious research into the problem is conducted. Indeed, the more that is learned about the Year 2000 Problem, the more probable it becomes that it will be a full-scale disaster.

What Does The Government Say?

Numerous Congressional hearings have been conducted by both houses of Congress and a major study has been done by the Congressional Research Service which is a department of the Library of Congress (a copy of the study report is included in Appendix B). Senator Moynihan (D-NY) requested the study in the spring of 1996. Here's a quote from the report,

> *Many managers initially doubted the seriousness of this problem. .... (I)ndependent research firms, however, have refuted this view. ... (T)he majority of US businesses and government agencies will likely not fix all of their computer systems before the start of the new millennium."*
>
> *Congressional Record, August 11, 1996*

Senator Moynihan sent a letter about the Year 2000 Problem to President Clinton in July, 1996. This is a quote from that letter (which is also included in Appendix B),

> *Dear Mr. President:*
> *... I write to alert you to a problem which could have extreme negative ... consequences. The 'Year 2000 Virus.' ... I first learned of all this in February (1996) and requested a study by the Congressional Research Service. The study ... substantiates the worst fears of the doomsayers. ...*
>
> *I am advised that the Pentagon is further ahead ... than any of the Federal agencies. You may wish to turn to the military to take command of dealing with the problem.*
>
> *The computer has been a blessing; if we don't act quickly, however, it could become the curse of the age."*
>
> *Congressional Record, August 11, 1996*

What Does The Press Say?

Here are quotes from prominent sources concerning the Year 2000 Problem.

> *"... for some institutions, ... it will soon be too late. We could end up with a real catastrophe that could affect many people's lives around the globe ... One industry expert has called the ... defect 'the most devastating Virus ever to infect the world's business and information technology systems.'"*
>
> *Washington Post, September 15, 1996*

> *"The (IRS) is launching a massive effort to forestall a breakdown of the income-tax system when (the year) 2000 arrives .... If the agency cannot quickly revise millions of lines of obscure software code, ... (it) will throw*

*the government's financial operations into chaos.
Computers throughout government and private industry face the same problem. ... (E)xperts say the federal government ... has been dangerously late in recognizing the ... problem"*
                    Los Angeles Times, October 16, 1996

*"Computer Flaw Threatens Havoc. In the silent
realm of cyberspace, a doomsday clock is counting off
the seconds ... (I)ndustry representatives warn (that)
computer users could find themselves with a giant
techno-hangover - when ... checks bounce, benefits are
cut off and taxes become immediately due. Anything
that depends upon software for its operations is potentially at risk. ... Even sprinkler systems and some state
buildings could shut down. If this problem is not ad-
dressed, nearly all computers ... could fail."*
                    Sacramento,Bee, July 14, 1996

What is Business Saying?

Major voices from business and industry are treating
Y2K seriously as well. They are saying such things as,

*"The world of finance ... is especially vulnerable. ...
(T)he absolute worst case ... is a global financial melt-
down' ... Clearing and settlement of transactions could
break down. Stocks held electronically ... could be
wiped out. Interest might not be properly credited ...
Deposits or trades might not be credited to an account.
... (T)he consequences may be catastrophic'"*
                    Business Week, August 12, 1996

*"Almost everyone who's looked at the problem
agrees not only that it's profound and potentially dis-*

astrous, but that no silver bullet exists to zap it."

Newsweek, January 20, 1997

Finally, in an exhaustive and well-known study, Capers Jones, the Chairman of SPR, Inc., a prominent Massachusetts-based consulting firm sums things up by characterizing the Y2K challenge as .....

"...the most expensive single problem in human history."

The Global Economic Impact of the
Year 2000 Computer Software Problem
Study published by SPR, Inc., Burlington MA, 1996

An Eye Opening Experience

I first became aware of The Y2K Problem on April 2, 1996 at a business meeting in Northern Virginia. Several speakers mentioned The Y2K Problem and I obtained a brochure about Y2K. I started researching the subject on the Internet that same evening and my life has not been the same since.

A month later, I attended a Y2K conference at the Department of Commerce in Washington, D.C. The title of the conference was, "The Millennium Time-Bomb." Some of the attendees were from industry but most were from the many government agencies located in the nearby Washington area.

At the end of the day, my head was swimming. One moment in particular really stands out in my mind. It was when the moderator asked the audience to indicate by show of hands how many agencies had started at least a pilot project to cure their Y2K situation. Of the 500 attendees, only a half dozen or so hands were raised. The moderator (who also chairs the government's inter-agency

Y2K Working Group) was visibly stunned and said, in shock,

"This is much worse than I would have imagined."
Kathleen Adams
Social Security Administration

At that moment, I realized Y2K was going to be a catastrophe.

What's In This Survival Guide?

Here is a preview of the remaining chapters of this Y2K Survival Guide:

What Is The Y2K Problem? The next chapter of this Guide describes the nature and severity of the Year 2000 Problem. It doesn't go into great technical detail, however, because I don't want to lose anyone in a boring technology discussion. For those who want more of this kind of detail, Appendix A provides a more microscopic approach. Chapter 2 also provides a detailed "schedule" of how the Y2K phenomenon is expected to play itself out. Several specific dates are identified when the probability of Y2K problems is particularly high. Critical preparations for the Y2K Crisis cannot be made without understanding the timing of the problem because many difficulties will occur long before the Year 2000 actually arrives.

Y2K and The Federal Government The third chapter describes the effects Y2K will have on federal government programs and on those who receive benefits from these programs. It concentrates on programs and agencies which have a significant impact on large numbers of citizens such as the Social Security Administration and the

Internal Revenue Service. Specific actions are recommended to help the reader set up protective measures against Y2K problems in the federal government.

Y2K and State and Local Governments Chapter 4 shines a harsh and penetrating light on those governments closest to you. Interestingly enough, there is more potential danger locally from the effects of Y2K than from federal sources. Detailed action steps are provided to show how the reader can survive glitches and outright failures in local government computers.

Y2K and Public Services Chapter 5 illustrates Y2K's possible impact on a broad range of public services such as police and fire protection, transportation, utilities, communications and health care. All forms of travel could be hazardous and many of life's necessities such as electricity, water and telephone service could be seriously impaired as Y2K develops. This chapter shows how to be ready if these disruptions in our social infrastructure do occur.

Y2K and Your Financial Affairs Chapter 6 details the terrible potential of Y2K on your financial well-being. It discusses such topics as insurance, investments, banking, mortgages and pensions. The protection of your financial assets is one of the fundamental goals of this Survival Guide. This key chapter shows you how to accomplish this important objective.

Y2K and Your Vital Information Information on you and your affairs resides in data bases everywhere. The seventh chapter examines these sources of data and how you can protect yourself from Y2K created problems with that data. Examples include college transcripts, credit reports, military service records, and voter registration records. Building a Y2K Shield around your vital information is essential to surviving the crisis.

Y2K and Employment Chapter 8 shows how your paycheck, benefits, payroll taxes, personnel records and your job itself could be negatively affected by Y2K. It also lays out specific steps you must take to ensure your employment data remains safe and how you can survive even if your job is destroyed by the Y2K Crisis.

Y2K and Your Personal Well-being The potential is high for extensive economic and civil disturbances brought about by Y2K related problems. I am not a "head for the hills," survivalist but I do recommend a number of personal safety steps the prudent individual should take. Chapter 9 lays out a basic plan for you and your family.

Legal Implications of Y2K The new century will see the greatest blitz of lawsuits in history. Chapter 10 will tell you about the Y2K "Ambulance Chasers" and who they will be going after. Action steps are provided to show you how to avoid becoming entangled in the coming legal chaos.

What You Can Do To Help Chapter 11 details things you can do to spread awareness of Y2K to others. It also shows how you can focus the attention of business leaders, public figures and government agencies at all levels onto the Y2K Problem. Public awareness is the most important weapon we have against the Y2K Challenge.

Conclusions The time remaining between now and the "roll-over" to the Year 2000 will be filled with chaos and uncertainty. Events will unfold rapidly and in many unexpected directions. The final chapter of the Y2K Survival Guide shows you how to keep up to date on the progress of the Year 2000 Problem and where you can obtain additional information on the subject.

Four appendices follow the main text of the Survival Guide. They contain the following information:

Technical Details Appendix A provides technical details about The Y2K Problem for the computer literate.

Sample Letters Appendix B contains sample letters you can write to spur public and private officials into taking action on The Y2K Problem. There are also sample letters you can write to private companies and to government officials demanding that the services and goods they provide are free of defects caused by The Y2K Problem.

Y2K Source Material Appendix C provides copies of some important Y2K source material such as an official report of The Year 2000 computer challenge, conducted by the Congressional Research Service in June, 1996.

Vendor Directory Appendix D is a directory of dozens of vendors across the United States who state they can provide you with the goods and services you will need in the event the Year 2000 Problem develops into an emergency situation where you are located. <u>I am not affiliated with any of these vendors.</u>

About The Author

Before I get into the details of the Year 2000 Problem and its effects, I want to give you a little information about myself. Parts of this Survival Guide are going to make me sound a lot like "Chicken Little," so this is intended to let you know I am a real person and not someone with some sort of hidden agenda.

I am a retired Naval Officer with 24 years active service who came up through the enlisted ranks. I spent my entire career in the electronics field, including a tour as the Electronics Maintenance Officer on an aircraft carrier. In that job, I directed 5 junior officers and 102 enlisted technicians and was responsible for the upkeep of 7,000 pieces of electronics equipment. At age 33, I earned a degree in Business, graduating with honors from the Naval Postgraduate School in Monterey, California.

In my civilian life, I have been involved in shipbuilding, communication systems design, satellite systems, software engineering, training and marketing. I also have extensive experience in computers and software. For two and a half years, I taught business courses at a local community college. I am currently working in business development for a leading software company in Northern Virginia. In summary, I have a strong, 37 year background in technology plus significant experience in business.

I have a large family of which I am quite proud. Married nearly 36 years, my wife and I have eight children and five grandchildren. It would be fair to say I am pretty intense about family issues. When I look at The Y2K Problem and its potential for harm, what concerns me most is the damage it can do to families. This has given me a strong motivation in writing this Guide.

Why This Book Was Written

I am writing this Survival Guide because The Y2K Problem scares me to death and I don't think enough is being done to prepare for it. The purpose of this book is to help you make those critical preparations. Here are the most important things I want you to know when you have finished <u>A Survival Guide For The Year 2000 Problem</u>:

1. How to protect your financial assets from Y2K related problems

2. How to safeguard your critical, private information from Y2K losses and contamination

3. How to protect yourself against the physical dangers caused by the Y2K Crisis

4. How to influence decision makers to take action on Y2K

There's More

The book you have in your hands is not all you will need to get through this crisis. In fact it is just the beginning. From now until after the Year 2000 arrives, I will also publish <u>Jim Lord's Year 2000 Survival Newsletter</u>, which will provide current information about the Year 2000 Crisis. If my book inspires you to take action to protect yourself against the ravages of this "techno-storm," you will need current information about how events are working themselves out. Indeed, the newsletter will be your most critically useful information as we move into the "eye" of the storm. Details on how to obtain the newsletter can be found on the order form in the back of this book, by calling my toll free telephone number (888-Y2K-2555) or by visiting my Internet site at www.Survive-Y2K.com.

Topics in <u>Jim Lord's Year 2000 Survival Newsletter</u> include:

- Federal government update

- State by state governmental scorecard

- Legal update

- Financial update

- Examples of Y2K problems experienced worldwide
- Y2K and the business world

- ... and many other useful and timely Y2K insights

Final Thoughts

My philosophy in writing this book is pretty simple and is based on the lessons learned by an old sailor with many years at sea. In particular ...

when a storm is coming - your best bet is to prepare for the worst.

Here is a "sea story" related to this thought. During the first few years of my shipboard career in the Navy, I will admit I thought some of the precautions we had to take while the ship was underway were a little silly. Using string to tie down lamps, typewriters and chairs seemed extreme to me. I guess most young sailors feel that way - until the first time they experience an unexpected, heavy roll. That happened to me <u>inside</u> DaNang Harbor when my ship took three monstrous rolls the last of which was nearly forty degrees. This harbor has a very long, slowly rising bottom. Preparing to set anchor, we turned slowly to come about into the seas. Just then, a set of heavy, rolling swells caught us exactly broadside. The first rolled us to starboard moderately and we then rolled back to port in recovery. Just as we rocked to starboard again, the second swell caught us exactly in sync and we went to starboard heavily. The effect was just like pushing a child in a swing. As we recovered from the second roll, the third and largest swell arrived and it almost turned the ship over. The effect was astonishing. We nearly capsized <u>inside</u> a harbor on a clear, calm day!

Most small items around the ship ended up dangling from those silly strings but many desks, file cabinets and workbenches broke loose and tumbled from one side of each space to the other. The major casualty was most of the glassware in the crew's galley and the officer's mess. There were no serious injuries but there were two lasting effects. A lot of young sailors became old salts that day and no more complaints were heard about preparing for heavy seas.

Some of the steps I recommend to you in this book will also seem silly or extreme. It is quite natural to ignore problems that are still on the far-off horizon. I freely admit I do not know if Y2K will only cause some disruptions here and there or if there will be an out and out catastrophe, so let me state the issue this way.

If a doctor told you there was a five percent chance you had a life threatening cancer, would you get an X-ray? To me, the answer is obvious. Of course I would. I see the Y2K Problem in exactly those terms but I believe the probability of deadly consequences is much higher than five percent.

Let me make this point clear; I am not an alarmist and the purpose of this Survival Guide is not to cause panic but to strongly encourage preparation. My greatest hope is that little of what I predict herein comes true. As each day goes by, however, I am more and more convinced that most of it will actually happen.

I am faced with the dilemma of trying to figure out how to get the audience to leave a burning theater. Whispering, "Fire!" has no effect whatever. Screaming "Fire," is also ignored because the tendency is to ignore hysteria. The fact remains, however, that the theater is on fire. The smoke and flames are not yet visible to most but, if you know where to look, the evidence is overwhelming.

The Year 2000 Crisis will be the most dangerous and widespread technical calamity ever faced by mankind. When a hurricane threatens, not even the experts can foretell exactly where it will strike and precisely how bad it will be when it gets here. Y2K, on the other hand, will strike everywhere in the world. All at once. Rich and poor; young and old; men, women, and children; guilty and innocent; the slothful and the fully prepared alike will all feel its effects.

I hope this Survival Guide inspires the reader to make preparations for this "storm," because, the wind is picking up and the sky is turning dark. And, in this case, I guarantee, this disaster will arrive exactly on schedule.

"Oh yeah, I'll tell you something,
I think you'll understand."

"I Want to Hold Your Hand" - the Beatles

Chapter 2

What Is The
Y2K Problem?

A Quick Experiment

From a technical viewpoint, Y2K is a simple problem that is quite easy to illustrate. Here's how. Pull out any major credit card and read the front. Somewhere on the face of the card will be the month and year the card expires. It will say something like "Valid Thru 9/97," which means the card is good through September, 1997. When you use a credit card, it is typically "swiped" through a reader which then "talks" to a computer. The computer checks three things: your name, the card number and the expiration date.

Now, imagine that same card with an expiration date of September in the year 2000. It will be stamped "Valid Thru 9/00" as shown in Figure 2-1 on the next page. This card will be <u>rejected</u> at many locations because some computers cannot process a year of "00" Although we humans would know what it means, computers can be confused and not realize that the zero actually means 2000. Instead some computers will think it means zero. (Imagine that!) Other computers will think it means 1900.

Until just recently, cards like this one were being issued all over the world. And thousands of them were being rejected as invalid or expired. In fact, at a conference I attended recently in San Francisco, at which a Vice President of Visa International spoke, I learned that most major credit card companies have stopped issuing cards that expire later than 1999 because there were so many problems reading them. They have managed to stick a finger into the leak in the dike, but are now scrambling to actually fix the problem all over the world.

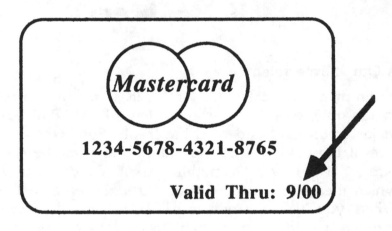

Figure 2-1

I'm sure it's pretty inconvenient to have a credit card rejected. I can imagine, though, how it might be a lot worse. Maybe you're trying to check into a hotel somewhere far away from home at ten o'clock at night after a long day's flight. And for safety's sake you don't like to carry a lot of cash. And you have a critical business meeting at eight the next morning. And ... but you get the picture.

Y2K Is Already Here

The credit card example above illustrates a very important fact. The Y2K Problem is not some far off problem that is going to suddenly pop up in the Year 2000. The fact is ...

The Y2K Problem is here right now !

Computer failures and calculation errors are already happening and we'll see more and more of them as we approach the end of the century. One of these problems will eventually result in someone's death. Sooner or later, another will cause a large company to fail. It might even be a bank or a stock exchange. We will also eventually see the failure of one of the major government agencies and the loss of the some government services. It will probably take a few of these kinds of events before the public starts to really catch on to The Y2K Problem and the grave threat is represents.

A Bedtime Story

The following story illustrates another very important aspect of Y2K.

I like to keep the heat down real low at night because I sleep better that way. This sometimes results in a very chilly bathroom in the morning, however, so I wear this big, thick, purple terry-cloth bathrobe.

Now, I really do like that bathrobe even though my kids tell me it's pretty ugly. But I don't care because it's very comfortable. Well, lately I've started having a serious problem with it. Some of the threads have started to unravel. At first it was just one. I pulled on it a little and, to my chagrin, I got a handful of crinkly purple thread.

I tried to find a place to pinch it off so I could break the thread but no luck. The more I pulled, the more crinkly stuff I had in my hand. I finally used my little scissors and cut off the thread real close. A couple of days later though the thread was hanging down again, and worse yet, more threads were showing themselves. Now I have to give my bathrobe a "haircut" every few days and I know this old friend is not long for the world.

The Y2K Problem is sort of like my old bathrobe. When you start pulling on a few threads you discover there is a lot more to this problem than meets the eye. You also discover that the problem could have cata-strophic results. The Y2K Problem is actually a "family" of about a dozen different date-related problems. The one I describe in the credit card example above is called the "two digit year" problem and although it is the most well known aspect of Y2K it certainly does not make up the whole of the Y2K Problem.

The Complexity of Y2K

The following is a simple listing of some of the other kinds of Y2K related problems. No details are provided here because I don't want to bog down this part of the Guide with a bunch of boring technical stuff. You don't need to understand any of the items on this list and you can just skip it entirely if it makes your eyes glaze over. It is included only to make you aware of how complex and how extensive The Y2K Problem is.

- Computer applications will process two digit years incorrectly

- Data containing two digit year fields will trigger computer calculation errors

- System clocks on many computers will fail to accurately "roll over" to the year 2000

• The Year 2000 is an "unexpected" Leap Year

• Many computer programs and some computer chips use a forced 19XX to indicate the full date

• The Y2K Problem extends to operating systems, application software, data, software development tools, compilers, networks, utilities and even some hardware

• Even if a given system is Y2K compliant, it can import "tainted" data from an outside source, reinfecting itself

• "Tainted" data can be imported over a network, infecting (or reinfecting) all attached machines

• Since many older data bases use "99" to signify End of File (EOF), records of individuals born in 1899 or in 1999 could create grossly inaccurate sorts and finds.

• Many older data bases use "00" or "99" to cause a record to be purged or to trigger some other logical process or action including shutting down the computer entirely.

• "Hidden" dates used in the makeup of serial numbers and inventory records will cause calculation errors which cannot be traced

For the technically minded , a more detailed explanation of each of the above examples is provided in Appendix A at the end this Survival Guide.

The Hard Part

This thing sounds kind of silly, doesn't it? Just two little digits. How could something so simple as a two digit
year cause such a serious problem? <u>The answer to this
question is critical,</u> for it is the key to understanding the
Y2K Problem.

Imagine this situation. You live in a beautiful village
in a lush valley beside a lovely river. The population of
your little community is just 500 people. Fifty miles up-
stream is a gigantic dam across the river. One morning
the dam gives way and a massive wall of water begins
roaring down the valley destroying everything in its path.
In two hours it will arrive at your village.

Your problem is simple. A great deal of water is about
to cover your village. The solution is equally clear. You
must build a high barrier of sandbags around the village.
Your engineers estimate one million bags will do the job
but that's just a rough guess. As luck would have it, there
is a shovel factory and a burlap bag warehouse in your village. I won't bore you with the math, but, each and every
person in the village must fill, carry and stack two thousand sand bags during the next two hours. That works out
to about one sandbag every four seconds. Pretty grim,
huh?

There are two unknown factors at play in our little
drama. It is not certain how deep the water will be or how
high you'll be able to build the sandbag barrier. Both factors will determine how much damage will be done by the
flood. If you start right now and do everything exactly
right, maybe you'll only get a foot of water into the village. On the other hand, you might be facing a catastrophe
no matter what you do.

Lets recap. You understand the problem clearly and

you know exactly what needs to be done to fix it. You have the required tools and all the necessary materials. These might not matter, however, because what you lack is time and people to get the job done.

The above example exactly describes the Y2K situation. The technical experts completely understand Y2K. They know how to fix the problem and they have all the tools and materials they need. But that's not enough because ...

> Y2K is not a technical problem. It is a management problem of monumental size and complexity

In fact, like the floodwater problem described in the story above, the Y2K Problem is so tough it can no longer be solved in the time available to work on it.

How Big Is It?

Efforts have been made by academics, consulting companies, trade associations, professional societies and the government to estimate the size of the Y2K Problem. In general, they agree on these two essential points. The problem is huge and their estimates probably aren't very accurate. It's sort of like asking how many gallons of water are coming down the valley from that broken dam. The only answer with any real meaning is - more than enough! There is a certain consistency in the results that are coming out, however. Most of them are saying, "It's worse than we thought at first. It's harder and more costly and takes longer than we expected."

One reason these estimates are so "fuzzy," is that most companies and government agencies don't know how much software and how much data they own. Software is intangible. It can't be seen, heard, weighed, smelled, tasted or felt. It can be copied easily and repeatedly. It can be transferred to any place on the face of the earth or even deep into outer space in an instant. Counting software is like counting thoughts. Or dreams.

Another reason there is little hard information is very few businesses and government agencies have started to seriously attack the problem. Most of what we do know is pretty scary, however. Here's one example. A well-known railroad realized their budgeting and scheduling software (which uses future dates) was giving them incorrect results. After an exhaustive study, their project leader said,

> "To convert these programs, we estimated that it would require ...100 staff years. The problem turned out to be much larger than we had realized."
>
> Charles Parks, Union Pacific Railroad
> *Datamation* ,Jan 1, 1996

Some well known studies estimate there are about 250 billion lines of computer code that need to be inspected and repaired. About 80-90% of all software programs will require some sort of repair. Global cost estimates range from $300 billion to $1.3 trillion. The U.S. Government's share is estimated to be somewhere between $30 and $75 billion. No money has been budgeted, however, so this cost will have to come "out of hide."

The Time Crunch

The only way to make sense out of these numbers is to consider the time factor. So what does the time-line look like?

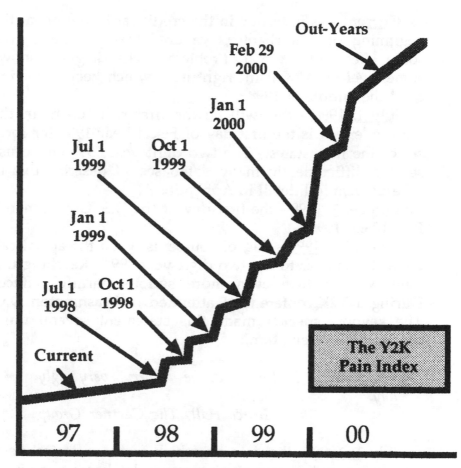

Figure 2-2

As indicated earlier, Y2K is already here but there are some specific dates coming when there will be "spikes" in what I call the "Y2K Pain Index." Figure 2-2 above illustrates this concept. In the chart, the years are shown across the bottom and "Y2K Pain" goes upwards along the vertical axis.

Here is a brief explanation of each part of the Pain Index.

Current - as indicated in the credit card example at the beginning of this chapter, we are already experiencing some effects of the Y2K Problem. The diagram shows some level of "Y2K Pain" right now which keeps growing until the middle of 1998.

July 1, 1998 - this will be the first real "ouch" in the pain index. It is the first day of Fiscal Year 1999 for forty six of the fifty states. The two digit year "99" will cause serious difficulties in many databases. I describe this in greater technical detail in Appendix A.

October 1, 1998 - the first day of the U.S. Government's Fiscal Year 1999.

January 1, 1999 - this, of course, is when the actual calendar turns over to the two digit year "99." Reaching this date will produce even more serious harmful effects. During a Y2K conference I attended in Washington D.C. The keynote speaker made this statement several times during his presentation,

> "January 1, 1999 will be a very, very ugly day."
>
> Bruce Hall, The Gartner Group

July 1, 1999 - the date on which forty six states' fiscal year becomes "00" causing even more databases to go nuts.

October 1, 1999 - this is when the federal government's fiscal year rolls over and becomes "00." With four spike dates, the year 1999 will definitely not be a good year. As before, the reasons are detailed in Appendix A.

January 1, 2000 - this will be the big one, naturally. Up to this point it has been data and software programs going haywire. As the calendar "rolls over" to the Year 2000, it will be the computers themselves going crazy. Millions will start producing incorrect date calculations and others will just simply quit.

February 29, 2000 - yes, even leap year is going to cause problems. For reasons I discuss in Appendix A, the Year 2000 is an "unexpected" leap year. By that, I mean it is, indeed, a leap year but many computer systems will incorrectly think it is not. By this time, I predict we will all be pretty numb, so this one probably won't create much of a stir.

Out-Years - this part of the chart represents the next ten years or so after the year 2000. Why does the Pain Index continue to rise even after we arrive at the end of the century? Shouldn't it fall? The reason is, by this time, Y2K lawsuits will be in full bloom. Believe me, if you got tired of OJ, wait until Y2K litigation hits full stride. Imagine - Y2K Ambulance Chasers.! Many large law firms are already forming Y2K litigation teams. They see that huge pot of gold sitting out there. Some estimates indicate the litigation will cost as much as One Trillion Dollars! I will discuss this topic in greater detail in Chapter 10, The Legal Implications of Y2K.

The dates in the above Pain Index where the line shoots up sharply are what I call "Spike Dates." These occurrences are very important because they are specific dates when there could be major disruptions going on all over the world. In the following chapters, I will provide action steps you can take to help protect you and your family from Y2K related difficulties. Each set of action steps will start with specific "Spike Date" action steps.

A Thousand Sand Bags

Now that you have a feeling for the time-line aspect of the problem, let's go back to the cost for a moment. Remember that estimated cost range of from $300 billion to $1.3 trillion? Match up that number with the period of time left before the real "ouch" in the Y2K Pain Index arrives. Here's the question. How can you spend that much money in such a relatively short time period? Again, I won't bore you with the math. The answer is you would need over <u>800,000</u> software professionals working on the problem full-time starting immediately. To put that number into perspective.....

That's over 40% of all the software professionals in the United States.

And that's the minimum. Obviously, if the actual cost is at the high end of the range, the problem would require more than one hundred percent of all the software people in the U.S. Which brings me to the most important point of this chapter.

Can We Get There From Here?

Many experts are beginning to consider this important question. Their conclusions are certainly not comforting. The chairman of a prominent professional society stated in a recent newsletter,

"...Are we already too late? Is it even possible to (fix) all of the date problems in essential business systems and mission-critical software? ... We need some careful thought about how much of a fix is good enough to avoid wholesale business loss and economic chaos."

Eliot Chikofsky
Software Engineering Technical Council

In my research and in my professional contacts in the software industry, the constant refrain is Y2K may be bigger than we can possibly solve in the time available. Believe me, this is not an isolated thought. Recently, my boss was told by a very senior government official that

Y2K could not be solved within the U.S. Government no matter what action is taken. We have already run out of time. That dam up the river has already broken and the water is on its way.

Why Y2K Is So Severe

The Y2K Problem is best understood by recognizing it is essentially a massive information contamination problem. To demonstrate the importance of this problem in the big scheme of things, let me discuss just a little bit of basic economic theory.

Traditional economic thought identifies three fundamental components of all economic systems. In the text books, these are called "factors of production" and they include:

Land. The earth itself plus the improvements to it such as roads, bridges, buildings, electrical power, and water.
Labor. The mental and physical efforts of human beings.
Capital. The money and the devices it can purchase which accomplish work in substitution of human beings. This factor includes machines and computers.

In an industrial society, these three factors were considered to make up the essential ingredients of all economic systems and all economic analysis for many years consisted of evaluating these three components.

Recent economic thought adds an additional factor to this list - information which I define here as an intangible commodity which has economic value over and above its physical nature. A book, for example, consists of the physical components of paper, ink, glue and perhaps a little cardboard. The value of these physical things, even new, might be fifty cents or a dollar. Why are we willing, then, to pay twenty five dollars at the book store for the latest bestseller? It is because of the high value we place on the information contained between those cardboard covers. Information can be printed, of course, but it can be even more intangible than that. All the worlds computerized databases and computer programs are also information. So are the electronic signals we send flying round the globe on satellites and into our living rooms to entertain and inform us.

Consider the peculiar business of billionaire, Bill Gates, President of the Microsoft Corporation. First, he buys little, three inch wide plastic disks (called floppies) for a dime apiece. Then he hires tens of thousands of very bright, young people and throws them into a big room with the floppies and lots of pizza and Coke. After a while they return the little floppy disks to him and he sells each one for a hundred bucks. The amazing thing is those little disks have exactly the same weight and physical appearance as when they went into that big room. The only difference is they have had added to them that which has more value than any of the other factors in the modern economic system. Information.

The reason Y2K is such a serious problem is that it attacks this fundamental component of the modern economic system. For comparison, imagine the effect if one of the other factors of the economic equation began to turn rotten. Consider how it would affect the economy if the very earth itself became contaminated and useless for any purpose. That is the effect Y2K is having on information.

Accurate information about you is crucial to your well-being because society, especially government, uses this information to monitor and/or regulate behavior. It is also collected, processed, reformatted, bought and sold as a precious commodity in the marketplace. This book will attempt to demonstrate how crucial the commodity of information has become in our world and how seriously this commodity will be impacted by the Y2K Problem.

The Global Perspective

It is important to recognize that we live in a vast and interconnected global economy. Much more so than many people are aware of. There are several important considerations. The first is that fixing the problem here in the United States does not fix it in the rest of the world. As poorly prepared as we are in the United States, the rest of the world is lagging sadly behind us in working on the Y2K Problem. What will be the impact on the United States if Asia, South America, Europe and especially Mexico don't get their computers fixed on time?

Down Mexico Way

We are heavily dependent on the vitality of the Mexican economy. After Japan and Canada, they are our third largest trading partner. The President and the Congress both understand how important this connection is. A couple of years ago when the Mexican economy was on the brink of failure, President Clinton unilaterally sent more than twenty billion dollars to Mexico to rescue them from bankruptcy. Although this action was legally questionable, congressional leaders in both parties put up no fuss because they all clearly understood the immense negative impact on our economic prosperity of a failure in the Mexican system. So they held their noses and propped up what many thought was a corrupt Mexican regime.

Unhappily, this strategy won't work when it comes to Y2K. First of all, we're too late. We are behind in solving our own problem and we certainly won't get around to helping Mexico until it is way past meaning anything. Secondly, money won't solve this problem like it did the previous one. Y2K takes skilled people, time and good management. Mexico will find it immensely difficult to marshall these resources. Accordingly, I believe Mexico will be a Y2K basket case and their failure will eventually come rolling across our southern border. It will have great negative consequences here, particularly in the border states of California, Arizona, New Mexico and Texas.

Will Europe be Ready?

Another consideration is that the European community is in the midst of adopting a new unified currency. Their target date is January 1999 and they could hardly have picked a worse time to make such a change. The European financial community (banks, stock exchanges, government regulatory agencies etc.) has thousands of programmers busy trying to prepare for the conversion. They should cancel this effort and become fully engaged with making Y2K software repair efforts. It will be a great political challenge for the politicians of all the countries involved to terminate the currency conversion effort and switch to Y2K instead. If they cannot bite the bullet and alter their course it will greatly intensify their Y2K Crisis.

The Hong Kong Connection

As this is written, Hong Kong is part of the United Kingdom. In July, 1997, however, the colony will revert to the control of the Republic of China after 156 years of British rule. The effect of this reversion on the Asian and global economies is uncertain because of the secretive nature of the mainland Chinese government. Whether they will allow Hong Kong to continue as one of the world's least regulated and highest-flying economies is unknown.

This much is known for certain, however. Hong Kong will go through significant social, economic and political changes over the next several years and these changes will occur during the greatest technical crisis in world history. I could not begin to predict what the outcome might be but trying to manage the repair of all the Y2K impacted computers in Hong Kong while all these other things are happening will greatly complicate their situation. In my judgment, the potential for serious Year 2000 difficulties in Hong Kong is very high.

I'm Ready if You Are!

The remaining chapters explore the effects Y2K might have on you and your family and how you can protect yourself from the Y2K Crisis. We look first at federal government programs.

Chapter 3

Y2K And The Federal Government

Imagine

Government spending constitutes about a third of all economic activity in the United States. Every nickel of that amount is processed over and over by a multitude of computers all of which are susceptible to the Year 2000 Problem. All government services from the military protection we enjoy to the weather forecasting we depend on are managed by computers as well. What might happen to our society if those computers get sick and begin to malfunction? Let's see.

Your mom is frantic. She called you at work this afternoon and pleaded for you to come to her apartment at the retirement village right away. After your father died three years ago, she moved into the village because several of her friends were there. Her Social Security checks plus the modest pension your dad left provide enough for her to live in relative comfort.

There isn't much left over each month so you help out from time to time. You wish you could do more but, all in all, she gets by pretty well..

At the apartment, she shows you the registered letter she received that has her so upset. The letter is notification from the Social Security Administration that her benefits have been terminated effective immediately. Your heart nearly stops but there is more. The letter goes on to say that all benefits received in the past 12 years (nearly $150,000) were received fraudulently and must be repaid with interest. You search your wallet for that business card from your lawyer,hoping this thing can be resolved easily but knowing there is a good chance you have a long, hard (and expensive) fight ahead.

The next day you get your own bombshell in the mail - a terse letter from the Internal Revenue Service. The letter says their records indicate you have failed to file a tax return for the past three years. You are directed to appear at their offices ten days from now at 2:00 PM with all financial records for the time period in question. They state that an attorney is not required but one is highly recommended. A few minutes later as you discuss the matter with your accountant on the phone he says, "You know, something funny must be going on. You're the third client this week who got this same kind of letter."

As you drive to his office, you hear on the news that civil disturbances are going on in the streets in Detroit and that a whole set of government weather satellites are going to fail because of some sort of computer software problem. "Can't those idiots get anything right?" you ask yourself.

Will Washington Fail?

The federal government is not ready for the Year 2000 Crisis and there is only a slim chance it will be ready. This is not just a guess, it is the government's own admission. Senator Moynihan of New York recently tasked the Congressional Research Service to conduct a study to determine the impact of the year 2000 Problem on the federal government. The report (which can be found in its entirety in Appendix B) reads, in part,

> "...the majority of ..... government agencies will likely not fix all their computer systems by the start of the new millennium."

Another indicator of the federal government's readiness for Y2K is to be found in a recent survey of the Y2K status of twenty four major government agencies conducted by the House Committee on Government Reform and Oversight. Letter grades from "A" to "F" were awarded based on several factors including whether or not the agencies had a plan in place and whether they had made a cost estimate of their Y2K exposure. Fourteen of the twenty-four agencies were awarded letter grades of either "D" or "F." One agency did not even respond to the survey. Here is a quote from their report on the survey,

> The Committee ... is deeply concerned that many Federal Government departments and agencies are not moving with necessary dispatch to address the year 2000 computer problem. Without greater urgency, those agencies risk being unable to provide services or perform functions that they are charged by law with performing."

Like Molasses

The government's sluggishness in dealing with Y2K has several causes.

First, the politicians in both parties are motivated by staying in power instead of solving problems. They can be counted on to do exactly what is necessary to keep themselves and their party in office. Sometimes that primary motivation even results in a little progress for the country.

A second reason is politicians (just like you and me) tend to pay close attention to those things that bring them pain. One of the unfortunate characteristics of the Year 2000 Problem is that it's not causing much pain at the moment. Think back for a moment to the broken dam story from the previous chapter. Even though the flood waters are coming, the birds are still singing and the breezes are blowing gently. Everything seems perfectly normal and there is certainly no pain at the moment.

Such conditions make it very difficult for a politician (and many others as well) to get all worked up about the problem. Put differently, it's tough to put your game face on when there's no opponent in sight. While that is the case, the Year 2000 Problem will not receive much serious attention from the elected politicians. In all likelihood it will take the failure of a significant institution such as a major bank for the politicians to really get with the program. Meanwhile, that water is still rushing down the valley.

Thirdly, Y2K is going to cost a lot of money and the two parties are deadlocked in a budget fight. Neither party is likely to recommend spending up to 75 billion dollars on Y2K. One Deputy Assistant Secretary, described Y2K as a "forcing issue." That is, it will force the cancellation of many marginal programs in order to divert funding into critical programs. I suppose this will be one of the long-term benefits of Y2K. It will finally make us get rid of some of that fat. The hard way.

Fourth, the government won't be able to compete with industry for computer programmers who are already starting to become scarce. As this Survival Guide is written, some computer programmers are being paid $50 an hour. This has doubled in the last six months and is expected to double again in the next six months. The government simply cannot process its own red tape fast enough to keep up with this sort of trend. The government's own programmers will flee in droves in order to make $100 an hour and up - several times what they can make in government service. Then the government will get to hire them back as contractors at sky high prices, further exacerbating their own budget problems.

Finally, and most importantly, all governments are naturally slow and inefficient. In the United States, inefficiency is built right into the Constitution in the checks and balances (and resulting tension) between the three branches of government. The founding fathers knew very well that high efficiency results when power is concentrated in the government. But they also knew that concentrated power creates corruption and abuse so they willingly made the sacrifice. Our system is designed to avoid corruption but at the price of inefficiency.

Please understand, I'm not complaining about this system. It is necessary for it to work this way. If it didn't, those rascals in Washington would have things fouled up a lot worse than they are now.

The Government Machine

This chapter will be easier to understand if the reader thinks of government as a machine with inputs and outputs. Consider a lawn mower for comparison. It consumes gas and air (inputs) and produces a spinning blade (output). If any one of these inputs or outputs is disturbed in some way, the machine will not operate properly. For example, the lawn mower will malfunction if the gas flow is shut off or if it is restricted, or if it becomes contaminated with water.

The diagram below shows the government machine has two inputs, Money and Information and there are three outputs, Money, Information and Services.

Just like with the lawn mower mentioned above, if there are problems with any of these inputs or outputs, the government machine will malfunction. Unfortunately, all of them will be seriously affected by Y2K.

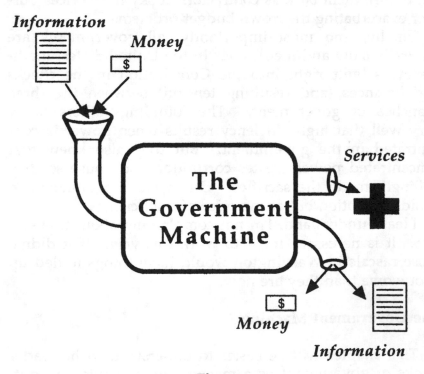

Figure 3-1

The Money Funnel

Money comes into the federal government from many sources but most of it comes directly from business owners, large and small. According to the Statistical Abstract of the United States, out of every dollar that flows into the funnel, about:

- *39 cents comes from personal income taxes*
- *32 cents comes from other payroll taxes such as Social Security, Medicare and Unemployment Insurance*
- *11 cents comes from corporate income taxes*
- *9 cents is borrowed and*
- *9 cents comes from excise taxes, customs duties and other miscellaneous sources*

The first three items on this list total 82 percent of federal revenues and they are all payments made to the government by businesses. Specifically, this is money that is paid directly to the Internal Revenue System.

This is a problem because multiple computers are used for every single payment. First, the business writes a check using its own computer. The check is mailed to the IRS which processes the check on its computer. The money is then sent to the Treasury Department which processes the check on yet another computer. The check then is then processed by a Federal Reserve Bank on a fourth computer which sends the check to the bank used by the original business where the check is processed on yet another computer.

In actuality, the process is more complex than this simplified description and involves several more computers than described above. The troubling fact is many of these computers could be crippled by the Year 2000 Problem. A failure in just one will disrupt a transaction and literally millions of transactions are made daily in sending money to the federal government. The Internal Revenue Service is the thin neck of the funnel. More than four out every five dollars coming into the government is stuffed through that one little bottleneck.

Tremendous disruptions will occur if the IRS computers have serious difficulties. Is this possible? It may be inevitable because the IRS has very old computer systems and notoriously bad management of their information systems in general. They have been trying for years to upgrade their systems but have botched the effort so badly Congress recently threatened to take the job away from them and give it to the Department of Defense! Moreover, the IRS has started very late in solving their Y2K problems. Y2K is a tremendous threat to the federal government because of the almost certain inability of the IRS to deal with the coming problems.

One of the possible impacts of Y2K on us common folks will be an increase in IRS errors in processing tax paperwork. Returns will be lost and payments will be misapplied. Erroneous tax liens will be placed on property and enforcement measures in general will become more draconian. It will be increasingly difficult to deal with the IRS because the very tax information itself will become corrupted. I talk more about information problems later in this chapter.

The worst thing that could happen to the money input would be for the IRS's computers to break down completely. If this happens, they will be unable to bring all that money into the federal government. On a personal level, this might sound pretty good but if it actually happens, it would be catastrophic because it would also mean government payments would stop. This possibility is discussed in the next section . Also, at the end of this chapter

I discuss steps you can take to help protect yourself against these possible IRS mistakes.

The Money Spigot

Let's follow the flow of money all the way through the machine to the output side which is equally suspect. The disruption of payments from the federal government is probably the greatest single danger from Y2K. A break-down of the expenditures themselves tells why (source: Statistical Abstract of the United States).

Out of every dollar the federal government spends:

- *22 cents pays for Social Security*
- *19 cents pays for other entitlement programs such as Medicaid, food stamps, pensions etc.*
- *17 cents pays for education, training, science, technology, housing, transportation, foreign aid etc.*
- *16 cents pays for national defense*
- *15 cents pays the interest on the national debt*
- *11 cents pays for Medicare*

Every penny of this firehose of cash is processed with computers and every penny is threatened by Y2K.

Social Insecurity

The two items on the top of the list above make up about 41% of all government spending and are called entitlement payments. Which means Congress does not have to approve the spending year by year. Instead, these programs are funded by existing (and perpetual) laws on the books. Recipients are simply entitled to receive the money by these automatically invoked programs. Social

Security is the largest of these programs and makes up more than half of the total. Every month, the government machine mails out an amazing 43 million Social Security checks totaling more than 30 billion dollars.

The Social Security Administration started working on Y2K in 1989 although it was the mid nineties before their software repair efforts kicked into high gear. In January 1996, they estimated 300 manyears were still needed to solve their Y2K problem the end of 1998 (three months after the first Spike Date!). Six months later, the estimate increased to 400 manyears. As is typical with most major Y2K repair efforts, initial estimates fell short of the mark. Will they finish on time? That's anybody's guess, but their trend line is definitely going in the wrong direction.

What if they don't make it? The disruption in payments could range from a modest blip to a full-blown catastrophe. If a blip occurred which involved just one percent of Social Security recipients, nearly half a million individuals would be affected across the country. Unfortunately, many Social Security recipients live from day to day on a very meager income and would suffer significantly with even a one month interruption in payments.

At the other end of the scale, a complete breakdown of the system is possible with terrible consequences. If this level of problem occurs, fully one sixth of the population of the United States would experience some sort of disruption of their primary source of income. Many months might be needed for a recovery. The consequences would clearly be catastrophic.

The Welfare Bomb

Almost one fifth of all government expenditures are welfare related and most of this money pours into the inner cities. A major disruption of this flow of money poses a great physical danger to millions of people. The Los Angeles riots several years ago were sparked by the acquittal of the policemen who beat Rodney King. It is difficult to imagine the conflagration that is possible if welfare money is disrupted across the entire country. These civil disturbances are possible if there is even a perception the money might stop. Chapter 11 discusses this side of Y2K in more detail and provides specific actions to be taken to prepare for the worst eventuality.

(Note: terms such as "welfare recipient" and "inner city poor" are sometimes used as code words to mean people of African American descent. I intend no such meaning in my usage of them. I am trying to help all who will be affected by Y2K. I assure you, Y2K is completely color blind, even if our society is not.)

(In)discretionary Spending

Nearly one third of federal expenditures goes to what is called discretionary spending which is split about equally between military and non-military programs. In this section I will discuss only the non-military half because military spending is covered later on in the section on government services.

Discretionary spending simply means Congress has to approve the expenditure every year in the annual budget A dizzying variety of things are included in this part of federal spending. A brief sample includes:

- *Student loans and grants*
- *Foreign aid*
- *Scientific research and development*
- *Space program*
- *Housing programs*
- *Highway funding*

- *Arts and humanities*
- *Disaster relief*
- *Loan guarantee programs such as VA and FHA*
- *Agricultural subsidies*
- *Government services such as national defense, weather, air traffic control, and law enforcement (discussed elsewhere)*

This list could easily go on for many pages but it doesn't need to in order to make this essential point about government spending.

Here's a key point - every penny of this 1.8 trillion dollars a year is somebody's income. And every bit of it is processed by computers which are, in many cases, old and mismanaged and, in all cases, prone to fail or make errors due to Y2K.

The fact is, if you receive money from the government for any purpose or if your employer receives money from the government for any purpose then your paycheck is at risk. If you are a student, a farmer, a government employee, a government contractor, or a treasury bill holder your income is subject to disruption or termination when Y2K strikes. Likewise, if your customers or your employer's customers are paid in any way by the government, your income is in jeopardy.

For these reasons, it is easy to understand why the expenditure side of the government machine poses such a serious concern.

Information Please

In the government machine diagram, information and money flow through the same pipeline. An examination of information flow through the government machine might seem like a strange topic which has little consequence for the ordinary citizen. Let me assure you, it is at least as important to you as understanding the money flow.

Here is a very important concept in this book.

Computers and high-speed, global communications have altered the fundamental nature of money. In today's computerized society, money is just a specialized form of information.

Remember those computers used to process money going into the IRS? They don't process greenbacks. They process financial information in the form of electronic signals. It is a fact of modern life that most financial transactions are done electronically through the use of "information-ized money." As one writer has said, money has become information and information has become money.

Even small businesses pay their employees using electronic deposits. We pay our bills with checks which are processed electronically. Most casual and personal spending today is done with credit or debit cards. Even gas pumps and pay phones these days take an electronic card. All of these mechanisms are used to convert currency and coins into the more convenient and powerful digital signals.

Two hundred years ago, 25 cents was referred to as "two bits." It is ironic that today, the smallest piece of electronic information used by a computer is called a "bit."

The Information Tax

Once you accept the idea of money as a specialized form of information, the concept of taxation takes on a new meaning. Not only do federal, state and local governments take our money in the form of taxes, they also extract a heavy information tax on the American people. Some of this "Infotax" is taken by force of law and some is taken as a condition of receiving benefits from the government. Yet more is simply taken directly by the government itself. This section will give examples of each of these forms of the Infotax and examine the impact each has on the reader.

The income tax return (as opposed to the tax money itself) is one of the primary means by which the government collects the Infotax on individuals, corporations, partnerships, individually owned businesses, trusts, estates and even on tax free organizations such as churches and charities. This information is coerced from the providers by force of law. If you refuse to comply with the government's demand for your information, they can send people to your house with guns. This clearly demonstrates how valuable the government considers this information to be. It is not necessary to either owe or pay monetary taxes to be subject to this use of force. If you engage in financial transactions, even if they carry no tax consequences, the IRS wants to know about it so they can put the information into their databases.

In addition to income tax returns, other forms of coercive, information gathering activities by the government include Social Security card applications (SSN's were formerly required in order to gain employment, now they are required on income tax returns for dependents one year or older), currency transaction reports (for cash transactions exceeding $10,000), Selective Service registration records and customs declarations. And then there is the greatest Infotax of them all...

The Red Tape Infotax

On an individual basis, an infotax is paid every time we use a government benefit or take part in any sort of transaction with any government entity. It is commonly called <u>Red Tape</u> but it works just like a tax. Here are just a few examples of the infotaxes that are collected and stored by government computers:

- *Census information*
- *Student loan applications*
- *VA and FHA loan applications*
- *Military service records*
- *Farm subsidy applications*
- *patent, trademark and copyright applications*
- *small business loan applications*
- *security clearance forms*
- *Immigration and naturalization records*
- *Passport records*
- *Federal court records (bankruptcy, trials etc.)*
- *Health records*
- *Pilot license records*
- *Financial disclosure records of federal office seekers*
- *FBI fingerprint records*
- *Veterans Administration records*

This list could go on for many pages but you get the picture.

Y2K and the Individual Infotax

Your personal information has great value to you and the Y2K Crisis threatens the validity and even the existence of that information. Take just a few examples from the above list to see what might happen. Then go back and see what sort of impact it might have on all the rest of the items in the above list.

- *student loans might be erroneously forgiven (good) or the amount due might become huge and overdue (bad) or, student loans applications could be lost or eligibility could be denied accidentally*

- *eligibility for veterans benefits could be lost*

- *passports could become invalid when they are indeed valid*

- *health records at federal facilities could be accidentally purged or eligibility for treatment could be accidentally lost*

- *Farm subsidy payments could terminate before eligibility expires*

- *eligibility for VA or FHA loans could be inappropriately denied*

- *Patent, trademark and copyright records could become hopelessly tainted*

In other words, if you are eligible for any federal benefit or try to obtain any federal service, it could be denied to you because of data residing in government databases which become tainted by the Y2K Problem.

The Business Infotax

The Infotax that is imposed on business is massive and costs businesses many billions of dollars every year. This cost is, of course, added on to the cost of all products and services and then passed on to us, the consumer. Some estimates are that this red tape costs the economy about ten percent of the national income. In other words about ten cents of every dollar you spend goes to cover the cost of the red tape involved with getting that product into your shopping basket. Here are just a few examples of the kinds of infotax the government imposes on business.

- *Securities and Exchange Commission (SEC) filings*
- *Occupational Safety and Health Administration (OSHA) reports*
- *Environmental regulation compliance reports*
- *Pension plan filings*
- *Equal Employment filings*

Y2K and the Business Infotax

All this information flowing into the government is processed by computers at either the business originating the information or the government agency receiving it or both. Accordingly, Y2K can have a serious impact on the flow and accuracy of the information. The results will be that information will be lost, corrupted or halted altogether.

So what? How can it harm us common folk if the red tape going to the government gets fouled up? The answer is subtle and critical to our well being. When the information goes sour, the government will lose its capability to effectively regulate industry. Even though the information is unreliable, the government will continue to try to use it and the misdirected and incorrect enforcement efforts will cause paralysis in the economy. The government will harass and shut down businesses and the economy will suffer because of it.

Additionally, many businesses exist just to gather up this red tape information, repackage it and sell it back to us. Those businesses will begin to have a difficult time when the information starts to become unreliable.

The Information Firehose

On the output side of the system there will also be problems. Information coming out of the system will also be corrupted, disrupted or terminated. Here are just a few of the government organizations that have a significant mission to provide information to the government or to the public.

Government Printing Office
Census Bureau
Library of Congress
US Geological Survey (maps)
Office of Consumer Affairs
Bureau of Economic Analysis
Patent and Trademark Office
National Institute of Standards and Technology
National Technical Information Service
National Energy Information Center
National Library of Medicine
Bureau of Labor Statistics
Consumer Product Safety Commission
National Archives and Records Administration
United States Information Agency

In addition to these, most departments of the government structure have some sort of regulatory power and publish boxcars of regulations which apply to their "constituencies." (But that's another book.)

Government Services

The federal government provides an astonishing array of services to the public. These services are provided by several groups of people. First are full time government employees, both civil service and members of the armed forces. Secondly, many services are provided by contractors hired by the federal government. Here is a listing of some of the more important services provided:

Military Services
National Security, CIA, NRO,
Global Positioning System Satellites
Weather satellites
Hurricane forecasting
Court system
    Supreme
    Circuit
    Appeals
    Tax
Law Enforcement
    Federal Bureau of Investigation
    Drug Enforcement Agency
    Bureau of Alcohol, Tobacco and Firearms
    US Marshall Service
Federal prisons
Customs Service
Immigration and Naturalization
National Park Service
National Forest Service
Disaster relief
Space program
Coast Guard
Hospitals ,VA and Public Health Service
Agricultural inspection

Scientific standards, time, etc.
Engraving and printing of money
Public Health Service
Centers for Disease Control
Department of State
Postal Service
Intelligence Services

All of these services are dependent on computers, of course, and they would be impacted in two important ways by the Year 2000 crisis. First, the services they provide could be disrupted or halted altogether when the computers start going crazy. This means anyone who is dependent on the services they provide will be affected. Here are some examples of what might happen:

*   *Military readiness could become dramatically undermined as weapon systems become unreliable or malfunction.*

*   *Many satellite systems could fail or become unreliable because they are critically dependent on accurate time and date in order to maintain correct orbits. These include weather, communications, navigational, surveillance and weather satellites. For example, the Global Positioning System (GPS) which provides navigational and time information commercially is already known to have a serious date related problem in most ground receivers.*

*   *Weather services could be disrupted affecting shipping, agriculture and other industries dependent on accurate and timely weather information.*

- *Court services could become unreliable having negative effects on the dispensation of justice and the resolution of disputes.*

- *Prisons could both release and retain prisoners erroneously.*

- *Law enforcement activities could become less effective.*

- *Hospitals could misdiagnose and inaccurately treat patients.*

- *Postal services could be slowed or severely disrupted affecting all aspects of the economy.*

- *Immigration and naturalization services could experience problems. The issuance and maintenance of passports might also become unreliable.*

In addition to the curtailment of services, government employees and contractor personnel could lose employment. Obviously, if you are a government employee or a government contractor or if you live in a locale which is heavily dependent on government spending, you could be devastated when the above kinds of services are disrupted.

Action Steps

In this and each of the following chapters of the Survival Guide, the reader is provided with tips on how to avoid or minimize Y2K problems. These will be concrete steps that can be taken to help protect you, your family or your business from the effects of the Y2K Crisis. Specific precautions concerning events on and around Spike Dates will be discussed first. If you remember from the second chapter, Spike Dates are specific times when Y2K problems will be especially intensified. This will be followed by more general actions you should be taking on a continuing basis. These are called "Continuing Precautions."

On occasion, I will designate an especially important step as a <u>Critical Action Step.</u> These are the most important things you can do to protect yourself from the Y2K Problem. If you chose to take any actions to protect yourself they should be these critical precautions. Seven Critical Action Steps are provided by this Survival Guide.

Spike Date Precautions

In general, try to avoid all transactions with the government on or around Spike Dates. If you have to send either money or information to the government, protect yourself by sending it a month or so before a Spike Date or wait until a month or more afterwards. This includes items such as tax returns and loan applications (student, VA, FHA, small business etc.). If possible, don't apply for a passport or a farm subsidy or for any government program on or around Spike Dates.

If you are receiving money or information from the government try to time its delivery so as to avoid Spike Dates if you have any control over the situation.

If possible, avoid using government provided services on or around Spike Dates. Don't depend on the postal service. Try to reschedule court appearances or doctor or hospital visits or treatments.

If you are a business owner, try to time the filing of required regulatory reports so they do not coincide with Spike Dates.

Don't start or terminate military service or government employment coincident with Spike Dates.

Continuing Precautions

Critical Action Step # 1
The Y2K Shield

This is the <u>most important single protective measure</u> discussed in this book. The Y2K Problem is essentially a massive information corruption problem. The reason it is so serious is that it attacks this fundamental aspect of our economic system.

Since your vital information is going to be disrupted, corrupted or lost due to Y2K, you need to somehow protect and preserve its integrity. You need a Y2K Shield. You can do this yourself by becoming your own librarian. You must start immediately to collect a hard copy of all information concerning you, your family and your business. <u>Obtain and keep paper copies of everything</u>. You will hear me say this over and over in this book. It is important. <u>Please do it.</u>

Start your personal documentation library now before the rush begins. Make up a list of all information concerning you and your family that might be in the hands of any government agency or other entity and then systematically try to get hard copies of that information. There is an excellent book which can help you in this task. Written by Matthew Lesko, it is entitled <u>Info-Power III</u>. In it the author tells how you can obtain just about any information in existence. (leading to another Critical Action Step).

Critical Action Step #2 -
Buy Lesko's <u>Info-Power III</u>

Buy this book now and use it as a guide to help you identify the critical information you will need. It can be found at any good bookstore. Simply reading through the book will cause a small bell to go off reminding you of information you should be collecting. It also provides names, addresses, telephone numbers and instructions on how to obtain the information itself.

The following are examples of some of the information you should try to obtain (remember, it is critical for this information to be on paper):

Military Service Record
Hospital medical records
Last seven years tax returns
Loan applications (student, VA, FHA, small business etc.)
Court records (bankruptcy, trial, judgments etc.)
Passport records
Selective Service records
Social Security Statement of Benefits Earned

In general, the more important any single piece of information is to your well-being the more you need a paper copy of that information. This topic is so imporant, this Survival Guide devoted an entire chapter to it.

"I think I'm gonna be sad,
I think it's today, yeah."

"Ticket To Ride" - the Beatles

Chapter 4

Y2K And State &
Local Governments

Imagine

Unhappily, state and local governments are lagging behind the federal government in their Y2K preparations.
There are some exceptions as noted below, but most of
them have been late getting on board the train. Additionally, state governments administer many federal government programs and cannot do some of their Y2K work
until the feds give them guidance which is late in coming.
Many state databases contain information vital to your daily welfare and the potential for difficulties on this front is
very high. How might these difficulties affect you personally? The following vignette will shows how.

What a hassle! It's six o'clock on a Tuesday
evening and you've just arrived in Atlanta on
business. You've been flying all day and you're
bushed. First thing tomorrow morning, you
have a business presentation to give to a major
prospect and you're loaded with sales materials.

You need to get on the road because you have an hour's drive yet to get to your customer's location.   But here you are stuck at the counter of this blasted rental car company.   You had a reservation but, for some reason, their computer won't accept your perfectly good driver's license.   You know it's good because you just got it last week.   You've checked with all the other rental car places in the airport but it's so late, none of them have any cars left.   As you ponder a huge cab fare, you wonder if that goofy expiration year of "00" has anything to do with your problem?

Two hours later and almost $200 poorer, you call your spouse to let her know you arrived OK. As if the day wasn't bad enough already, she has terrible news.   A certified letter from the county tax assessor arrived today.   Those clowns down at the courthouse have placed a tax lien on your home for failure to pay your property taxes for the past five years.   With penalties, they claim you owe them over $16,000 and they are notifying you the property is going up for auction if the bill is not paid.   This is all crazy, of course, because your property taxes are paid by the bank that gave you your home mortgage.   Could the bank have screwed things up that badly?   You know when you get home you are facing a battle with the bank and tax people.   Just what you need.

As you drift off to sleep in your room, there is something on CNN about how all the voter registration records in Arkansas have been contaminated somehow and how everybody there is going to have to register over again.   You chuckle, perversely delighted to see somebody else having problems besides yourself.

Good News and Bad News

The city of Phoenix, Arizona, became aware of its Year 2000 Problem early in January, 1995 when a judge sentenced an offender to five years probation (expiring in January, 2000). When a clerk entered the information into a computerized database, the court system's mainframe computer system crashed "hard down" as they say. (As an old electronics maintenance type, I have a feel for this kind of thing!) Phoenix was lucky because they knew they had a serious problem. It could have been much worse. The computer could have accepted the information, made a <u>hidden,</u> erroneous date computation and kept right on working with the bad information.

All kinds of unpleasant things could have resulted. Prisoners could have been released early or in error. Others deserving of release could have been kept beyond the end of their sentence. As things worked out, Phoenix assigned a Year 2000 team and started an extensive and well-thought out Y2K recovery program. As this Survival Guide is written, they are diligently plugging ahead and expect to be ready for the next century.

The states of Nebraska, Minnesota and California are also making some early Y2K progress. Nebraska saw the problem early and diverted a four cent a pack tax on cigarettes to raise money earmarked for Y2K recovery. Minnesota and California have set up state-wide Year 2000 projects and have started an inventory of all the computer software being used by the state.

In spite of this progress, politics still plays a role. For example, the <u>Sacramento</u> <u>Bee</u> newspaper in July, 1996 (as this is being written) had a front page article which reported that the state of California was just then becoming aware of their serious Y2K problem and wondering how they are going to pay for it. (Certainly not a popular notion in an election year!) The article went to state that agencies would have to bite the bullet and find the funding within their existing software maintenance budgets to fix Y2K. Makes you wonder what kinds of other services will be canceled to pay the Y2K bill doesn't it?

The bad news is that's about it as of the summer of 1996. Most of the rest of the state governments have done little to nothing or have just barely started. To be fair, I do expect other states to start taking action on the issue soon. The hard questions are, of course, will they do enough and will they do it in time?

The Federal-State Conduit

Individuals like you and me will be affected seriously by the inability of state and local governments to handle the Year 2000 Problem. The damage could even be greater than that caused by the federal government side of the situation. There are several reasons for this. First, a huge amount of the money spent by the federal government is actually spent via the states. In many cases, money is just sent to state agencies so they can manage the expenditures.

Here is one example. The state of Texas currently receives about $1.25 billion a year in the form of block grants for use in the following programs: Transportation, Job Training, Education, Community Development, Community Services, Energy, Child Care, Drug Abuse, Mental Health, and Aid for the Homeless. Federal legislation is under consideration to add Medicaid, Aid to Families with Dependent Children, Welfare, Child Protection, Food Stamps, Aging, and Housing programs to that list.

The trend in Congress over the past few years has been to expand the transmittal of federal money to the states. In 1995, about one sixth of all federal spending ($225 billion) was sent straight to the states. The problem with this approach from a Y2K perspective is that it adds more layers of computers into the equation, all of which are prone to year 2000 problems. The states have become an ever expanding conduit through which federal funds are pumped. In Chapter 3, government was compared to a machine where disrupted flows in any part of the system would create problems throughout. Having the states so solidly plugged into the flow of federal funds will increase both the chances and the severity of federal Y2K problems.

The Smaller They are, the Harder They Fall

Another reason state and local governments will probably have a more difficult time with the Year 2000 Problem is because they have a greater resource problem than the federal government. For example, states, counties and cities can't just print money the way the feds can if they run out. Additionally most states have strict balanced budget laws they have to adhere to so they can't borrow their way into a solution the way the federal government can. Finally, even though the federal government is behind the curve when it comes to Y2K, the smaller government entities are even farther behind and when the competition really heats up in the hunt for programmers to fix the problem, the feds and the commercial world will get there first. This will leave the local governments in a distant third place and fading.

They're Everywhere, They're Everywhere

Here is an amazing fact (from the <u>Statistical Abstract of the United States</u>).

There are about <u>90,000</u> state and local government entities in the United States.

Most of these governmental units are not especially sophisticated computer users. They don't have extensive information systems staffs. When the Y2K Problem starts to manifest itself in ever more serious ways, these folks are going to have a very tough time of it. This is a serious danger to ordinary citizens on an individual level because these small governments have custody of massive amounts of information that are critical to your well being. The rest of this chapter will look harder at this information and how it could be impacted by Y2K at the state and local level.

Who Are You?

Your very <u>identity</u> is jeopardized by Y2K.

In America today, the Driver's License is the most commonly used piece of personal identity documentation. We are commonly asked to show it to cash a check, take a commercial airplane flight, or close a real estate deal. It is so important to us that the Driver's License Ordeal (DLO) has become a part of our social fabric. We all remember what it was like to get this cherished little piece of paper the very first time. It was important to us because, as teenagers, the driver's license symbolizes freedom and is <u>the ticket</u> signifying passage from childhood into adulthood. As the father of eight children, I have a lot of DLO experience.

As time passes, the DLO takes on a new meaning. Every few years, each of us has to make the dreaded renewal visit to the Department of Motor Vehicles or whatever the agency is called in your state. As adults, the DLO comes to symbolize something entirely different. Today, for adults, it has come to represent the "Incompetent Bureaucracy." We all have our favorite story of standing in line for what must have been hours just to have some petty, uncaring, power-crazy ~~jerk~~ clerk treat us like "some kind of second-class citizen." (don't get me started here!)

What's the Y2K connection? Simply this - in most states, driver's licenses are highly automated and thus are routinely processed by computers. In Maryland where I live, for example, driver's licenses have a magnetic stripe on the back just like a credit card. (Remember the credit card in Chapter 2?) And guess what - in many cases, the expiration date is recorded using just two digits. Y2K is already causing driver's license related problems today. I have twice heard at Y2K conferences that both Hertz and Avis have turned away customers because their computers rejected driver's licenses expiring in the year "00".

Another way Y2K will affect driver's licenses is that every state uses a computerized database to store and process driver information. Those computers are susceptible to Y2K difficulties and, as we get closer to the millennium, will make more and more Y2K related mistakes. Holders of valid licenses can be lost from the system. Renewals can be erroneously denied. False criminal charges could be filed. It is even possible that some states' systems could crash altogether just like the court system's computer in Phoenix.

Need a Ride?

Automobile registration records will also be a source of Y2K problems. Imagine this scenario: a gaggle of boisterous teenagers are driving dad's car which is the same make and model of a recently stolen vehicle. An idle cop with nothing better to do runs a license plate check on the car. A computer with a Y2K problem mistakenly indicates the license plate is invalid. Can you finish this story in several ways ranging all the way from the merely unpleasant to the completely tragic?

On a larger scale, databases used to store and process automobile registration records could cause grief for many states. The problem is made even more complex because the databases are often connected to other state agencies; federal law enforcement agencies such as the FBI, DEA, BATF and the Federal Marshal Service; auto clubs such as AAA and finally, insurance companies. This means errors in the database could be fed along the line to all these other users. This kind of interdependence of databases and diverse, multiple users is very widespread and will greatly exacerbate the Y2K problems to come.

State and Local Revenues

Y2K will affect the collection of income tax revenues for state and local governments in exactly the same fashion as it will affect the federal government. In addition, the smaller governmental units have numerous other sources of income all of which will be affected by the Year 2000 Crisis. The loss or disruption of this income means the government would not be able to spend money on popular programs or upon highly desirable services normally provided by the government such as fire, police, emergency medical and infrastructure related services such as roads, water, sewage etc. The effect of Y2K on these public services is covered in the next chapter.

Virtually all states and counties collect property taxes all of which are calculated, tracked, billed and posted on computers. All conceivable kinds of Y2K related errors could occur as we approach and enter the next century. You could be simply billed for the wrong amount. The error might be small or run into the millions. You could, for example be incorrectly charged for eighty or ninety years worth of back interest for unpaid taxes. Or, alternatively, the error could run in your favor. Large property owners could even experience huge tax relief windfalls. It is also possible that large, inaccurate liens might be placed automatically against your property. In the massive confusion surrounding Y2K, there will likely be out-of-state or unsophisticated property owners who lose their properties to the government for erroneous nonpayment of taxes.

State sales tax collection could be affected because payments received by the government from businesses might be "lost" due to inaccurate posting. Businesses might then be charged by the government with non-payment of taxes. Tax collection abuses by governments at all levels will very likely grow.

State-run lotteries will not be immune from the effects of Y2K. One lottery, in Arizona, failed in 1996 because the computer system used to record and track sales state-wide was incorrectly programmed and did not recognize February 29 as a leap day. The day's income was lost to the state and the contractor that operated the lottery was fired. Fortunately, the income was later recovered from the contractor's insurance company.

In summary, every source of income to all levels of government is in jeopardy because of Y2K. If government can't get money, it can't spend any unless it borrows or makes its own (applies to federal only of course).

Mountains of Paper

Public records and vital statistics are also in jeopardy due to the Year 2000 Problem. Some of these important personal records are maintained in computerized databases and many are still maintained in paper form. Even the paper-based records are not safe from the effects of Y2K, however, because even though the document itself is on paper, virtually all states use databases to keep track of and manage the mountain of paper. The documents themselves might be OK but nobody would be able to find the right piece of paper. Here is a brief list of the sorts of public records which could be affected.

- *Birth certificates*
- *Death certificates*
- *Marriage licenses*
- *Divorce records*
- *Name change affidavits*
- *Voter registration records*
- *Business licenses*
- *Drivers licenses*
- *Driving records*
- *Automobile, boat and airplane registration records*
- *Hunting and fishing licenses*
- *Incorporation records*
- *Court proceedings*
    judgments and liens
    civil cases
    criminal cases
    adoption records
    juvenile records
- *Property tax records*

- *Real estate records*
  deeds
  mortgages
  plat maps
- *Planning and zoning records*
- *Inspections and permits*
  well
  sewage
  building permits

Action Steps

Spike Date Precautions

A set of special Spike Dates exists on dates on which the fiscal year begins for each of the fifty states. Each state has its own particular Spike Date associated with its own fiscal year. There is an important national consequence, however, because forty six of the fifty states use the same date - July 1st.

Here are the fiscal year start dates for all fifty states.

New York	*April 1st*
Texas	*September 1st*
Alabama and Michigan	*October 1st*
All 46 others	*July 1st*

The importance of these particular Spike Dates is that they could cause Y2K problems so much earlier than most people expect. July 1, 1998 marks the beginning of fiscal year "99" for forty six states. That is when many older databases will experience the "99" problem and begin to malfunction. (Review Chapter 2 and Appendix A for more detailed information on this particular aspect of the Y2K Problem.) This could be an important early indicator of how serious the overall Y2K problem might be on a worldwide basis. It is also the date by which most of your preparations should be completed.

As advised in the previous chapter on the Federal Government, try to avoid all transactions with state and local governments as well on or around Spike Dates. Review the precautions from that chapter and follow the equivalent actions on the local level.

There are a number of additional precautions you should take regarding state and local governments, however. Don't get a driver's license close to a Spike Date. Additionally, check your license now to see if it expires during the years 1999 or 2000. If it does expire then, try to get it reissued so it expires in 1998 or even in 2001. (This assumes we will all have the Year 2000 problem solved by then.) It may be that you will even have to "lose" your license and get it replaced. This might cost you a few dollars but at least you won't get stuck later on with a license that some computer will reject. Also be sure to check your spouse's license and those belonging to any children or parents who drive.

Avoid registering cars, boats or planes on or close to Spike Dates. As above, try to avoid licenses that expire in either 1999 or 2000 even if you have to get them replaced.

Don't file your tax return or pay property taxes close to Spike Dates. Try to file or pay far enough in advance or after Spike Dates so that any computer glitches will at least be known about by the time they process your return or payment.

Avoid all legal transactions during the time period surrounding Spike Dates. This includes real estate closings, trials, hearings, affidavits, marriage, divorce, adoption, name changes, filings to comply with government regulations, business license application, incorporation, building permits, inspections of any kind and planning and zoning actions. In short, avoid government at all levels if possible.

Continuing Precautions

The Y2K Shield mentioned earlier is more important in regards to state and local governments than it is in respect to the federal government because local governmental entities store more information that is vitally important to you. This should be completed prior to June, 1998 which is less than two years as this survival Guide is being written. The June date is recommended so that you will have your campaign finished prior to the beginning of the "99" fiscal year beginning in most states (see above).

Review this chapter and the previous chapter to start on your inventory. Some of the critical documents you should get into your information library are your driver's license, driving records, auto registration and all real estate and legal records such as a court related stuff and marriages, divorces etc.

I will repeat here my suggestion of the previous chapter to get a copy of Matthew Lesko's book Info-power III and use it as a guide for the kind of information you need and the sources of that information.

Another strong suggestion is for each reader to embark on a campaign of letter writing to public officials about the Year 2000 Problem. I cover this subject in detail in a later chapter, but it is worthwhile to mention it here as well. This suggestion applies to federal government officials as well but it is the local guys who are most responsive to this kind of public pressure. In Appendix B of this Survival Guide you will find sample letters to write to some of these officials as well as mailing addresses of some key ones.

I also have an entire chapter on your personal information and how you can protect it. I will have more to say there on many of these subjects.

"There's a chance that we may
fall apart before too long."

"We Can Work it Out." - the Beatles

Chapter 5

Y2K And Public Services

Imagine

For convenience, I define public services rather broadly as those things we depend on everyday in our society but don't spend a lot of time thinking about until we need them. This includes the roads and bridges and traffic lights, buildings, elevators, electric power, water, hospitals, subways, trains and planes and emergency services such as the police and fire fighters. In short, I mean all those systems and people that make our society go and hold it together. Most of those things are operated or managed by computers and could fall prey to the Y2K gremlins. Here are a couple of ways this might happen.

It's like some kind of nightmare. Your normal thirty minute drive home took almost an hour and a half. The traffic lights were working at every intersection but their timing seemed to be all out of whack. <u>Every single light</u> was backed up for blocks even though there were no *accidents in sight. The whole city seemed to have become a slowly creeping parking lot.*

You had a dinner engagement with friends this evening and had to postpone because you got home so late. At one point, on the way home, you pulled off the road to call your wife to let her know you were going to be late. You couldn't reach her, however, because the operator said your phone was no longer in service. What the heck could be causing that? You're certain the bill was paid on time.

You're steamed as you sit in the car waiting for the next light and your ear catches something on the news about how massive power outages in New York City knocked all the stock exchanges out for the entire day and they still haven't been able to find out what caused the problem. Well, at least you're not the only one having a bad day.

Snow Job

The winter of 1995-96 was a pretty harrowing affair where I live, in Maryland. We experienced one of the the heaviest snowfalls of the century with drifts well over three feet. During one period we couldn't get out of the house for two days and then, when we got the driveway cleared, it did no good because the roads in and out of the subdivision were still snowed in. We even ran short of some "essential" food items such as eggs, bread and milk (to say nothing about chips and soda!). When we finally were able to get the car out and to the nearest grocery it was a madhouse with snow piled ten feet high in the parking lots and everybody trying to do the same thing we were. It was a full week before things began to approach normalcy. Now, we weren't in any danger of starving (I had some old crackers lying around) but we certainly did have a convenience emergency.

My sixteen year daughter did not weather the storm well at all. She was the proud possessor of a crisp new driver's license and had school concerns and a part-time job and a pressing social calendar. Not being able to get out of the house and take care of life's normal day to day activities was more than just inconvenient to her. It was plain frightening.

On one occasion, her best friend Loren, (also sixteen) was on her way to our house and skidded off the road and into a snow-filled ditch. The poor girl sat there with snow up to the windows trying to reach her family on a cellular phone. No one was home and her batteries began to die. Nearly hysterical, she reached my daughter but was unable to describe exactly where she was. Then the phone went out completely and my daughter joined her in hysteria-ville. So off we went into the storm to find poor Loren. After tracing every possible route between our house and hers we did finally find the car. But no Loren. She had managed to dig her way out of the car and had struck out on her own. The story ends well at this point because she had made her way to safety. The memories live on, however. It was a vivid lesson for my daughter because it was the first time in her tender young life that the public services infrastructure was not there when she needed it.

In a way, these public services are invisible. We take these things so much for granted that we don't pay any attention to them at all until something goes wrong. This is very dangerous because there is a lot of that infrastructure that is vitally important to us in our daily lives. This chapter will identify these invisible facilities and how they will suddenly become very visible when Y2K strikes.

Infrastructure Failure

Y2K could cause serious and widespread failures of the public service infrastructure of our daily lives. Part of what I mean by infrastructure is just what you would think - the physical structure such as roads and bridges. But I also mean public and private utilities such as electrical power and water, transportation services such as airlines and trains as well as emergency and safety services such as fire fighters and police. Most of these infrastructure goods and services are managed in some way by computers and all are potential casualties of the Y2K Crisis.

Let's Get Physical

Lets take the physical stuff first. I include in this category roads, bridges, tunnels, buildings, airports, port facilities, locks and dams, etc. I see three different kinds of Y2K-related problems affecting these physical parts of the infrastructure.

The first is maintenance. I spent a good many years of my military career working in this field and have a strong appreciation for what is involved. To keep mechanical things working, you have to prevent them from breaking by "fixing" them in advance. In other words, you seek out problems and repair them on your own time rather than after the equipment fails (which it will always do at the worst possible time. It's a law!). This concept is called <u>preventive</u> maintenance. Lots of factors are important in a good preventive maintenance program such as manning, spare parts, documentation and tools but the single thing that holds the whole thing together is <u>scheduling</u>. This is the factor that brings together at one time and place the equipment being maintained and the people, tools, information and materials required to do the job. Guess how most maintenance schedules are maintained in to-day's modern world? On computers, as you might have expected; computers which are prone to Y2K failure and disruption.

Maintenance difficulties will probably not bring the in-frastructure crashing down around our shoulders. The ef-fect is much more likely to be one of slow deterioration although there will eventually be instances of massive failures. These will be hard to pin on Y2K because poor or missed maintenance today might not cause a problem un-til next month.   It is a fact, however, that infrastructure maintenance will get worse as scheduling programs begin to fail. This will happen because automated schedulers process future dates and as we get closer to the turn of the century, more and more of these future dates will be "99" and "00" which will cause the problems.

Light of My Life

The second impact of Y2K on the physical infrastruc-ture is that a significant part of it needs to be operated and much of that operation is done or controlled by comput-ers. But how do you "operate" something like a road? Here is one example.

I live in Maryland to the east of Washington DC and work in Virginia just to the west of the city. Every day I get to drive right through the nation's capital. (This is a terrible punishment which I am certain I have done noth-ing to deserve!) Sometimes my drive is made very miser-able because of an accident somewhere on the roadways. On some days, instead of the normal 40 minutes to make the drive, it will take an hour or even more. Once it took two full hours to drive the 26 miles home. On occasion, however, the culprit is not an accident. It is, instead, a set of streetlights.   Sometimes these lights fail altogether (usually due to a loss of power) and eventually a trooper or two will show up and direct traffic through an intersection. Other times though, the lights themselves malfunction and this is usually much worse, especially when the lights lose their timing pattern altogether and revert back to flashing red in all directions. This means everybody has to make a full stop and then feel their way gingerly through the intersection. This condition never fails to produce spectacular traffic tieups in all directions.

Here is the Y2K connection. Many modern traffic lights are controlled by tiny computers. Many lights, especially at very busy or very complex intersections, are controlled by sophisticated and complex timing programs which alter the light's patterns according to the day of the week, the time of day and even whether or not it is a holiday. These control programs are very susceptible to Y2K errors. For example, these computers could believe that a weekday is a weekend or a holiday and change over to the weekend or holiday timing pattern. Or they could stop processing altogether and cause the lights to either turn off completely or revert back to flashing red in all directions

Now here is the scary part. It won't be just one single light. It will be hundreds or perhaps even thousands depending on where you live. And the problem will be very difficult to fix, because in most cases, the lights are not controlled by a central computer but by many smaller ones. Additionally, the governmental organizations that own them won't know they have a problem until it actually arrives. To make matters even worse, the problem will often cross a multitude of jurisdictional boundaries in major metropolitan areas. In short, my prediction is that you will see massive traffic jams all across the country caused by Y2K.

Hot, Dark and Sweaty

Here's another example of how infrastructure is "operated." I work on the seventh floor of a high-rise office building which is located in a virtual forest of high rise buildings in an area called Crystal City near the Pentagon. During regular office hours, I just walk through the building lobby and take the elevator up to the floor where my company is located. If I have to go into the office in the evening or on a weekend, however, I have to first insert a electronically coded card into a special card reading device that talks to a computer which checks the card's validity and then deactivates a door lock. It is also possible to get to these elevators through a wonderful underground shopping mall but after hours the elevator controls at this level are deactivated by that same computer. I'm sure you are starting to see the problem. The computer has a sophisticated date tracking software program that keeps track of the time of day and the date and whether or not it is a weekend or a holiday.

It gets much worse because access control systems are just the tip of the iceberg. In many modern buildings virtually everything is controlled by computers with date tracking software. Electrical service, lighting, water, sewage, air conditioning, heating, ventilation and even telephone service are controlled by date tracking computers. All of which are sensitive to the Y2K Problem. This part of the Y2K problem is not restricted just to office buildings of course. All kinds of facilities are impacted such as warehouses, factories, apartment buildings, retail facilities, churches and so on.

In my Navy days at sea, we would sometimes lose electrical power in parts of the ship which, of course, disrupts the lighting and the air conditioning. When this happened we would say we went "hot, dark and sweaty."

That's what is likely to happen to a lot of the physical infrastructure as a result of Y2K.

There's More

There is yet another aspect of the Y2K problem and its effect on the physical part of the infrastructure and that is the people and the organizations involved in its operation and maintenance. These could be governmental agencies such as departments of public works and highway administrations or they could be private, commercial operations such as real estate companies. These infrastructure owners all employ workers who need to be managed, directed and especially paid, functions that are universally accomplished with the use of computers. These organizations will, in and of themselves, be affected by the pervasive debilitation of the Y2K Problem. The computers that take care of their budgeting, planning, payroll, employee benefits, taxes, work schedules, personnel records, leave schedules and so forth will also get sick and cause the organizations to experience severe management challenges. They will likely become much less effective in their all their functions.

Now, I can tell you my friends, the thought of Washington DC becoming even less effective in filling pot holes is one very, scary thought indeed!

Utilities

The next piece of the public services infrastructure is public and private utilities such as electrical power, water, sewage treatment and communications services such as telephone, cable television and cyberspace. Everything written above about the physical infrastructure applies to this category as well. Utilities and facilities associated with them require maintenance, have to be operated and are managed by organizations full of human beings just like the physical infrastructure. (Please note that maintenance of nuclear power plants is a special consideration because of obvious critical safety considerations.) In all cases these parts of the infrastructure are controlled or managed by computers which will be affected by Y2K. There are some very important ways, however, in which they are different. So different, in fact, that they require separate treatment in this Survival Guide.

Fragile Networks

The first important difference is their unbelievable fragility which was dramatically illustrated just recently (summer 1996) when the western part of the United States experienced two massive power outages. The worst of the two extended from the Mexican to the Canadian border and from the Pacific coast to as far east as El Paso, Texas. In both cases, the outages were triggered by relatively minor equipment failures that occurred while system demand was extremely high due to heavy usage of air conditioning on very hot days. The term for this kind of failure is the "snowball effect." It is like starting a huge avalanche by rolling a single, fist-sized snowball down a mountainside. As with an avalanche, it was stunning that so huge a problem was caused by such a relatively insignificant equipment failure. (I guess I would describe fragility for our purposes here to mean the capacity for widespread service outages to occur as a result of small, localized equipment failures.)

The fragility of the utilities will be strenuously tested by the Y2K Crisis. Electrical power and telephone service are probably more susceptible than the other components and they are also the services that are the most critical.

Water and sewage treatment will also be affected but probably to a lesser degree because they are usually more localized in nature. All of these services are particularly Y2K sensitive because they are stringently controlled by date tracking software. For example, on weekdays, electrical power is increased to the workplaces such as inner cities and industrial areas. On weekends and holidays, however, the computers route the power to the suburbs where the people are. This automated scheduling of utilities will get out of whack when Y2K events strike. Massive outages will then follow because the systems are so sensitive to errors and will be overwhelmed by the widespread nature of the errors.

Pay Up Or Else!

Another major difference with utilities is that customers must pay for them, typically on a monthly basis. I would wager that not a single utility in the entire country is billed manually. Computers are used instead. Computers which are getting ready to go nuts because of Y2K. If the public and private utility companies do not cure their Y2K problems in these computers, incorrect customer billing will become widespread resulting in massive payment disputes. Service will undoubtedly be incorrectly terminated in many cases. Legal action will ensue. Faith and trust in billing will be completely lost and even more customers will refuse to pay. The utilities' cash flow will be disrupted resulting in even greater problems as employees go unpaid. In short, things could get real nasty just because the utilities can't keep accurate usage and payment records.

The Five Million Dollar Phone Call

Here is just one ugly little example. Let's suppose you decide to call your mom across the country on New Year's Eve just prior to January 1, 2000. You talk for twenty minutes and enjoy together the ringing in of the new century. Suppose you use that nice little long distance service that charges just ten cents a minute. You would expect to be billed a couple of dollars for the call. The computer, however, thinks you talked for a <u>hundred years</u> and sends you a nice little bill for <u>$5,256,000</u>!

That's almost as bad as my teen-aged daughter.

Cyberspace and Y2K

Just a quick mention about cyberspace service. In 1995, there were more E-mail messages sent in the United States than mail of all kinds through the Postal Service. In 1996 there will be more telephone service used sending data than sending voice conversations. Computerized communications has become much more than just a fad. It is everywhere and many, many businesses have come to depend on it as the primary form of everyday business communications.

Just a couple of weeks before this was written, a nineteen hour, nationwide service outage was experienced by America On-Line, the computer information service which has over four million users. It was the most serious outage ever experienced by any of the major computer information services. Blame was placed on human error when an engineer made some sort of mistake during the installation of some upgraded software. The story made the front page of all the major newspapers and was mentioned on every evening television news broadcast. One of the main points of the stories was the extent to which business across the country was so seriously affected.

These kinds of outages will become much more commonplace as Y2K problems increase with the approach of the next century. The on-line services as an industry are extremely vulnerable. Additionally, users of the Internet will find their favorite services unavailable or disrupted and billing for these services will be flawed for the same reasons as those stated above. Many companies are becoming addictively dependent upon Internet service. Indeed, the technology has spawned an entire industry that resides only in cyberspace. These companies are in particular jeopardy from the Y2K Crisis.

Getting Around

Transportation services and facilities such as airlines, trains, subways, bus systems, toll collection facilities and parking garages will also experience Y2K related problems. These kinds of systems also require maintenance and operation and will be subject to Y2K related problems in these regards. But there are also some special considerations which make them susceptible to problems in other ways.

One of the serious problems for the airline industry is the air traffic control system which is highly susceptible to Y2K problems. First of all, the system is very, very outdated. Some of the equipment, for example, still uses the old style glass, vacuum tubes which were old fashioned twenty-five years ago. The computer code is also very ancient and has been repaired (this process is called "patching" by the engineers) thousands of time. Along with the Internal Revenue Service, the Federal Aviation Administration has experienced extreme difficulty in trying to upgrade their computer software. Old fashioned computer code like this is very inefficient. It has been estimated, for example, that about one million lines of computer code are required just to get one plane from any city to any other city. The chances that this code can be safely used on or around Spike Dates is small indeed.

Long-haul transportation services like airline, train and even cruise ship services have naturally limited capacity. There are only so many seats or beds on that airplane, train or ship. The solution to this resource management problem is the widespread use of seating reservation systems. These systems smooth out the demand for services which increases customer satisfaction and makes the allocation of resources such as airplanes, flight crews and passenger train cars and engines more efficient. These reservation systems are, of course, managed by sophisticated computer software which is obviously intensively date related. Another aspect of this particular component of the long-haul transportation industry is the massive extent to which these systems are linked together by a world-wide network. All of the airlines and travel agencies in the world, for example, have access to the reservation database information from all airlines. That's how it is possible for your little, neighborhood travel agent in East Oil Slick, Arkansas to book you on a flight (including seat assignment) from Paris to Istanbul.

Sharing the Grief

My guess is the travel industry will be very hard hit by Y2K because of the global nature of the interconnected computer network used to manage reservations and schedules which are entirely date dependent. In technical terms, travel technology is extremely distributed in nature. That means the computers are spread all over creation instead of centralized in one or a few places. Every travel agent has his own desktop computer with its own software and they all tie into larger systems. This will make the Y2K problem very worrisome for these folks. And it is important to recognize that the problem will affect not only the "people mover" element (planes and trains etc.) but extends to hotel, rental car, resorts, conventions and all those other things that can be reserved.

What exactly will happen? If the problem is relatively mild, it will simply mean that travel reservations will be lost or canceled which will cost the travel industry money and result in widespread inconvenience for the customer. At the worst, extensive computerized database programs could fail outright, shutting down entire segments of the industry for days or even weeks. This would obviously have an extremely serious economic impact worldwide.

Buses and Subways

The localized travel segment such as buses, and subways will also have Y2K difficulties. Most of their problems will be related to the same aspects pointed out earlier in the section on the physical infrastructure, namely they have extensive equipment which must be maintained, they require extensive operation and they are also heavily labor intensive, meaning it takes lots of people to keep them going. All three of these involve heavy use of computers, of course. There is an additional aspect that makes them particularly susceptible to Y2K, however, and that is their heavy dependence on scheduling software which, of course, is entirely date related.

Parking Too?

Special notice should also be made of electronic toll systems and automated parking facilities. In one of my other lives, I spent some time in the parking industry with a company that manufactured parking computers so I can speak with some authority on this particular subject. I both designed and marketed these systems and can assure you these industries will suffer tremendously from Y2K. They consist of just a small handful of very specialized companies in an intense niche market. The equipment they manufacture is entirely dependent on date related software used to calculate fees over time. These systems will be prone to complete shut down. The facilities will respond by reverting to manual operation which will then cause customers to stack up in the streets.

Automated toll collection systems will be similarly affected. These are systems that outfit individual automobiles with electronic "tags" that are automatically "read" by a computerized scanning device allowing the driver to simply drive straight through a toll booth or gate without having to stop. Drivers typically pay on a monthly basis with a credit card. They are tremendously convenient for frequent commuters in major cities. The computer software that runs them is dependent on accurate date tracking, however, and will experience lots of calculation problems as the year 2000 rolls around.

If these last two problems seem unimportant, consider these two representative little factoids.

Oklahoma City's automated toll collection system has about one half million users

Philadelphia collects over $70 million a year in parking fees

Parking and toll collection are big business and play a major role in the financing and management of many large cities. Y2K will in no way be trivial for these types of systems.

Emergency ! Emergency !

The fourth and final infrastructure category includes essential emergency and safety services such as fire fighters, police, ambulance, hospitals and clinics, jails and prisons, and hazardous material management all of which will face their own special flavor of Y2K problems. Each of these has the standard set of considerations as mentioned earlier, those being maintenance, operation and personnel management. In general you can expect difficulties across the board with these. As before, what follows will detail the additional factors that make them special in some way.

Calling All Cars

The first three of these, fire fighters, police and ambulance are managed in a special way. They have to be dispatched to the scene of the emergency. For legal purposes, dispatching is an activity which is carefully recorded and monitored and universally managed by computer. An example of how tightly this computerized control is maintained was seen at the recent Olympic Games in Atlanta. When a bomb was exploded in the Centennial Park, the emergency dispatchers spent ten minutes trying to manually determine the correct address of the park. Since the park was brand new, it had not yet been added to their database. The heavy involvement of computers in these activities is a clear indication of Y2K sensitivity. Even 911 emergency calling systems are typically monitored, controlled and, most importantly, time and date stamped by computer. It is to be expected that some of these systems are highly susceptible to failure and disruption especially on and around Y2K Spike Dates.

Is There a Doctor in the House?

The potential for Y2K difficulties in hospitals, medical clinics and pharmacies is really scary. One of the central problems will be the databases which contain patient, treatment, insurance and billing information. Other problems will show up in the computer software using these databases. When these databases become corrupted you could begin to see patients treated for the wrong conditions or patients denied treatment because they get accidentally deleted from a database by either the hospital or the insurance company. Billing problems will also increase dramatically as patients are incorrectly billed, sometime in huge amounts. There will also be a rash of patient age-related problems as children are mistakenly treated with drug dosages intended for adults and elderly patients are accidentally sent to pediatrics wards. At its worst, there could be many deaths brought about by computerized medical malpractice which stem from Y2K-related problems in medical care facilities.

Crooks and Other Bad Guys

Jails and prisons will present us with yet another special flavor of the Y2K Crisis. I (thankfully) admit that I don't know very much about how these institutions are operated. I can guess, however, that they, like most organizations, have widely adopted the use of computers to help them manage most of their operational functions. I don't suppose they are any better or worse off than other kinds of organizations so I expect they will have just as many Y2K problems as the rest of us. What does make them different is that the damage that could result from their problems is severe in comparison.

Odds and Ends

Just a couple of items to mention here because they didn't really fit in anywhere else in this chapter.

First item - libraries will be devastated by the Y2K crisis. Their entire methodology of lending books and other items based on date is universally accomplished by computer. Libraries, except for the very largest, do not generally have significant Information Systems staffing and the funding of libraries is seldom adequate. These organizational deficiencies make them virtually helpless in the face of severe and widespread failures in their computer systems.

Second item - satellites. You probably don't appreciate how much you depend on these technical marvels but you probably use their services every single day. They play important roles in long distance telephone service, cable television and weather forecasting, for example. When you call Mom out in California, or use the Internet or watch CNN or check the weather for tomorrow's picnic, you are using services provided by those satellites. Many satellites are dependent on precise orbits for proper operation. This orbital maintenance is dependent on highly accurate date and time calculations which are done by computers both on the ground and on board the satellite. Many satellites also are dependent on precise location information relative to date and time. These satellites are also controlled and monitored by computers. In each case, the Y2K Problem has the potential to effect the correct operation of the system.

Action Steps

Spike Date Precautions

The Spike Date precautions you should take to protect yourself from public and private infrastructure problems caused by Y2K are simple to state but difficult to carry out. In a nutshell, avoid using the infrastructure on and around Spike Dates and take whatever actions you can in preparation for infrastructure failures.

Critical Action Step #3 - Stay Home

One of the key things I suggest is staying home on Spike Dates. This applies to your whole family, of course. By doing this, you will avoid traffic, road, building and public transportation-related problems as well as any difficulties experienced by the airlines, trains, etc.. You will also obviously be where you will be most needed in the event of massive outages - at home with your family. If you live alone, try to team up with someone. Being there to protect your loved ones and your property could be the most critical factor in getting through Spike Dates.

By staying home, I don't mean just staying away from work. Don't travel at all on or around Spike Dates and don't take a vacation either. You should not even make travel reservations on Spike Dates.

Double-check your bills for all utilities including power, water, garbage collection, sewage treatment, telephone, cable TV, etc. for months which contain Spike Dates. Be on the look out for erroneous billings.

Don't make telephone calls or go online on Spike Dates.

Stay out of jails and prisons on and around Spike Dates. In fact, this is a great recommendation for any time.

By all means, except for life-threatening emergencies, avoid medical treatment on and around Spike Dates and don't have any prescriptions filled then either.

Don't check out or return library items on Spike Dates.

Continuing Precautions

The Y2K Shield concept applies to certain aspects of the infrastructure piece of the Y2K Problem. Specifically, I recommend keeping hard copies of all utility type bills such as power, water, sewage treatment, garbage collection, cable TV, telephone, Internet provider, on-line service etc. They could be critical in helping to straighten our misbillings later or to prove (with canceled checks) that payments were actually made.

I also recommend that you maintain a thorough copy of all medical records. This includes a hard copy of treatment records from your doctor and from clinics and hospitals as well as all billing and payment data from treating facilities as well as from your medical insurance company. This will be a frustrating experience but could save your life (or your pocketbook) at a later date.

There are many personal well-being and safety recommendations I have to offer but they are sufficiently detailed and important that I have dedicated all of Chapter 11 to that subject.

"Who finds the money? When you pay the rent?
Did you think that money was heaven sent?"

"Lady Madonna" - the Beatles

Chapter 6

Y2K And Your
Financial Affairs

Imagine

This chapter investigates the possible consequences of
the Y2K Problem in the financial world which includes
investments, banking, insurance, pensions and mortgages
as well as other types of loans. Since all of these financial
activities are heavily computerized in today's modern
world, there is a strong possibility they will be affected by
Y2K. The sixty-four (billion?) dollar question, of course, is
how serious the impact will be. Consider for a moment
how such problems might influence your life.

It's very puzzling. You've had several tele-
phone conversations in the past half hour that
have left you wondering what could be going on
with your insurance company. A few days ago
your teenage son was involved in his first
fender bender.   A few minutes ago you took a
call from the other guy's insurance company.
They were trying to contact your insurance com

*pany and the number they called was not in
service. Figuring your son gave them an incorrect number in all the excitement you give them
the correct number. "No," the agent says, "that's
the number we're using and it's not in service."*

*Checking your Rolodex, you call your local
agent. No answer. What the dickens is going
on? After checking the policy for the telephone
number, you call the national office. And your
heart sinks.*

*A recorded message indicates the company is
taking no calls and instructs you to refer all inquiries to your state insurance board. This is
getting serious because your auto, life and home
insurance policies are with the same company.
Of course, you can always get insurance elsewhere but your whole life policy has built up a
value of over $50,000. Dreading what you are
going to hear, you place a call to the state insurance board.*

Watching the Dam Break

On both a global and a personal scale, the financial aspects of the Y2K Problem are simply terrifying. The mind
easily conjures up the Stock Market Crash of 1929 and the
Great Depression and the obvious question, "Could the
Year 2000 Problem be as bad as that?" The answer is, "Yes,
indeed." If the Year 2000 Crisis reaches its maximum potential, it could certainly produce the worst economic calamity in our country's history.

That's a pretty grim statement, but it is what could
happen if things end up at the worst end of the scale. I
feel certain we will experience at least major disruptions
in our economy. At the worst, I believe there is at least a

fifty-fifty chance the banking system will fail but I don't think that means a return to the dark ages. As a nation, we are pretty tough and amazingly resilient when things get really bad. I think we will work our way through this problem too, but not without a lot of heartache. Moreover, my purpose in writing this Survival Guide is not to just make a bunch of predictions concerning Y2K. I'll leave that to others with more expertise than I. What I am trying to do is make you aware of the problem and the range of <u>possible</u> consequences and to help you prepare for whatever does happen. I don't pretend to be an economic or a technological guru or prophet of any sort. I'm just the guy who is watching the dam break and, hopefully, has some understanding of what it means to the folks in that pretty little village down river.

Taking Stock

Corporate investments are the first topic and by that I mean things you can buy using a stockbroker such as stocks, bonds and mutual funds. Trading these kinds of investments makes you vulnerable to the Y2K Problem for two reasons. First, the investment industry is probably the most completely automated in the world. All transactions are handled by computer and each individual transaction typically involves several computers. It would not be unusual that a single trade would involve computers used by the following entities: the buyer, the stockbroker, the stock exchange, the buyer's bank, the stockbroker's bank and the stock exchange's bank. This is clearly a recipe for a Y2K disaster.

The financial industry maintains one of the most extensive databases in the world and every single record (or transaction) in every single data base is date coded. Every transaction must be "tagged" with the transaction date be-

----

cause the date of purchase is required by both law and logic.

Secondly, the financial industry is very likely the most extensively networked industry in the world. From a personal computer (sitting at the kitchen table!) in West Virginia, you can deal with a stockbroker in San Antonio, Texas, who can, in an instant, purchase the stock of a Canadian company on the Vancouver, British Columbia stock exchange and then make payment from a bank account in Switzerland using Canadian dollars into a bank account in New York City. Get the idea? This is a dazzling and wonderful capability but it horribly complicates the Y2K situation and makes the system vastly more vulnerable to worldwide problems.

The storyline of a recent Tom Clancy thriller, Debt of Honor, deals in part with sabotage against the computer systems used by the major New York Stock Exchanges. By bribing a computer programmer, the bad guys try to destroy Wall Street by contaminating the stock exchange's transaction databases. After the computer "bug" kicks in, all the data on each transaction is recorded correctly except one little piece. The three letter designation of which stock was purchased. In the story, this single little flaw threatens to bring down the entire economy of the United States.

Y2K, unfortunately is not fiction. It threatens the same kind of danger except that the computer system loses track of when transactions take place. The result would be equally disastrous, of course.

Let Me Count the Ways

Many kinds of errors could occur in the investment arena when Y2K strikes. Here is a partial list.

Incorrect dating. Correct transaction but credited to the wrong date. This would seem to me to be the most likely error.

Incorrect posting. You might buy a thousand shares and get credited with five hundred. Or five thousand. Or your purchase might be credited to the wrong account. Lots of possibilities here.

Incorrect billing. You might receive the correct stock but get billed in the wrong amount. Could be in your favor or not.

Incorrect balance. Calculation errors could result in improper dollar balance in your account.

Incorrect statement. Even though your account is actually correct, your statement could contain errors.

Incorrect deletion. Your records or individual transactions could be accidentally deleted. Obviously a disaster for you individually.

Temporary shutdown. One of the key computers in the chain could shut down entirely. Major inconvenience at the very least.

Database contamination or loss. Widespread database corruption could result in total loss for all or many accounts. Catastrophic because even the good data would then be of questionable quality.

Meltdown. System shutdown of long duration. Would probably result from software application *faults.   Obviously a major calamity.*

"I Know It When I See It."

Another consideration in the financial marketplace is going to be Y2K Compliance. The difficulty with this concept is that nobody knows precisely what it means legally. Not unlike the Supreme Court Justice who said he couldn't define obscenity but he knew it when he saw it! Accordingly, the government and the high-tech industry are flailing around trying to define the concept. Some government agencies are plowing ahead nonetheless and are using compliance statements without knowing just what they mean. The Department of Defense, for example, is sending a letter to existing contractors which includes the following paragraph,

> *"With regard to Contract number XXX please provide your certification, signed by the appropriate corporate officer, that all contract deliverables (both future and already delivered) are year 2000 compliant.   If they are not, please provide a detailed plan outlining what actions you will take to make all contract deliverables year 2000 compliant, which includes when these actions will be complete and all contract deliverables will be compliant."*

Boy, that ought to light up the lawyers. My guess is there will be some wrangling over the term and the Department of Commerce (or someone) will eventually come up with a "standard" definition and we'll have a Y2K Compliance Board of Inspection and so on.

On a personal level, in the next few years, the words "Y2K Compliant," or something similar such as "Y2KOK," will probably become as familiar on consumer products as

"Made in the USA." Some companies are already making plans to treat their early-in-the-game Y2K compliance as a market advantage. As this is written, I have already seen advertisements for one prominent company (Dun & Bradstreet) which tout the Y2K compliance of its products.

In Hiding

Here is an interesting question. If Y2K is such a threat to investments, how come there hasn't been much news about it? Well, for two reasons, the big companies don't want to talk about it. First, they don't want to reveal inside information and especially corporate weaknesses to their competition. Secondly, they know if there is bad news about their company, especially if it involves large increases in operating costs (such as funding the repair of millions of line of computer code), it will cause their stock price to go down.

Here is one example of how pervasive this reluctance is by some companies. Y2K support groups are being formed by software engineers and programmers all over the world who are trying to share information on how to fix Y2K problems. Reports are common that many large firms will not allow their employees to join these informal groups. On pain of termination from the company!

Even the mainstream press is minimizing the problem. For example, there is a prominent consultant, Mr. Peter deJager from Canada, who speaks all over the world on the issue and has also testified to the US Congress. He has been interviewed by the Wall Street Journal for an hour and a half about his prognosis for the Y2K Crisis. Not only have they not published the interview, they have yet to run any major articles about the problem. Is it because they fear such detailed coverage will inflame public passions and create a serious, perhaps even catastrophic effect on the stock market?

I believe this will change soon because of the influence of the big accounting firms. They will soon force the major companies to come clean on the effects of Y2K within their companies. (I cover this topic in greater detail in Chapter 10, the Legal Implications of Y2K.)

You Can Bank On It

Banking is extremely vulnerable to the Y2K Crisis for many of the same reasons as the investment industry. Banks for example, (and I'm lumping in Savings & Loans and Credit Unions here as well), are also highly automated and extensively networked. There are some important differences, however, which will be pointed out here. For one thing, the economic system itself is totally dependent on the <u>stability</u> of the banking system. The Federal Reserve system was created exactly for the purpose of maintaining that stability. The most critical factor in this stability is public confidence. From a Y2K perspective, this is also the banking system's greatest weakness because the Y2K Crisis will test this public confidence like no other event since the Great Depression.

The main problem is banks don't have enough money. Literally.

Imagine ten percent of a bank's customers showing up one morning to withdraw all their money. Suppose they refused checks and demanded the real thing, good old greenbacks. The bank could probably not accommodate even these few customers before it ran out of money. It would have to close its doors and declare a bank holiday. Then the fireworks would start. Word would spread like wildfire and there would be a panic run on the bank which means all the rest of the depositors would show up to get their money out too. This could lead to a more general panic that could spread to other banks and they too would start closing their doors.

Of course, the government will try to prevent this whole thing from happening and they might or might not be successful, but that is another story. Are bank holidays just a a figment of a fevered imagination? The last ones I know of in the United States occurred in the early 80's in Maryland and Ohio when a number of Savings and Loans were shut down. Because they were not federally insured, it was many, many months before all the depositors were able to recover all their money.

The Power of Doubt

It doesn't take a very big percentage of a bank's customers to start a panic because banks are only safe as long as people <u>perceive</u> them to be safe. The corollary is that banks can fail simply because people believe they might. This public perception of stability and safety is a whole lot more fragile than the government will admit. It is exactly here that Y2K is such a threat to the banking system. As an issue, it has the power to grab the imagination of the public and convince them their bank might not be a good place for their money. Amongst all the financial institutions, banks are the most vulnerable because we, the multitude, interact with them so frequently. If a problem does crop up, we will often learn about it within days or even minutes. The following section discusses some of the mechanisms through which we are "plugged in" to the banking system and its incredible computer network.

Chatting With the Bank

Many people talk to bank computers regularly and never give it a second thought. ATM's (Automatic Teller Machines) are a perfect example. These handy devices can be found just about everywhere from your local grocery store to a casino in Las Vegas. They are a perfect example of how heavily automated and how extensively net-worked our banking system is. ATM's are susceptible to the Y2K Problem in three ways. First, each one has its own small computer inside which processes transactions which use date information. Secondly, each one connects to your bank over a network (see the ACH section below for a more detailed discussion of this topic) which itself is operated by a nation-wide system of computers that track dates. Finally, your bank's mainframe computer (where your account information is stored) is susceptible in its own right.

Keep close tabs on ATM's and stories about them in the papers and on TV. If they have widespread problems, the story will be heavily reported and will be a certain in-dicator that the banking industry is having a very, very difficult time with Y2K.

Deal the Cards

I talked about credit cards in Chapter Two because they are so representative of the "plugged-in"-edness I men-tioned above. I haven't mentioned debit cards yet because in terms of Y2K they behave precisely the same as credit cards so I lump them all together here. Credit and debit cards are also indicative of how money is becoming "informationized" and information is becoming "monetized." When you mix these ingredients in with a nasty dose of Y2K, you get a very unpleasant mess.

The use of credit or debit cards may or may not result in a direct connection to the bank (or other institution) which issued the card. Some merchants are connected instead to a huge computer that keeps track of fraudulent cards, e.g. lost, stolen, expired or deadbeat. (One system I know of services over one hundred million merchants world-wide!) This can be done faster than a complete check of your name, card number and expiration date thereby speeding up transactions. At the end of the day, all transactions are "dumped" to a clearing house which sends them on to their respective banks.

This kind of fraud detection is commonly used by small ticket item merchants such as restaurants or parking garages. Large ticket item merchants such as department stores will use the other method of checking which is to go to a central processing computer which then goes directly to the issuing bank. This kind actually digs into your account information to see if you have sufficient "room" on the card to make the purchase. That is why getting your purchase processed at department stores usually takes longer than at restaurants.

This mix of methodologies seriously complicates the Y2K situation with credit and debit cards because there are so many players involved and each one has his own computer. Even though you may have only a single card, it can be processed by countless merchants using many different software programs with many central computing systems (again - see ACH below) before going directly to your bank. Much like a minefield, every step of the way is strewn with date processing Y2K bomblets. Growing credit and debit card rejections and inaccurate statements will be certain indicators of underlying Y2K problems with the banking system.

Making a Statement

Every month, account holders are provided with a snapshot of their bank account's status and a detailed record of all their transactions. This is the single most important measurement that can be taken as to the accuracy of the computing network behind the banking system because of the high degree of detail available. Missing and inaccurate statements will be sure signs that banks are experiencing Y2K problems. Missing statements, would, of course, be readily apparent but inaccuracy could be more difficult to detect unless the amount were very large. I have a friend who once discovered a $150,000 error in her favor in her bank statement. Interestingly, when she called the bank's accounting department to clear up the problem, they hung up on her, convinced she was a crank caller. The bank president did listen, however. (Very carefully, I might add.) Of course, you won't have to wait for your statement to arrive if the error is big and it is in the bank's favor. When your checks start bouncing around town, you'll know soon enough. Incidentally, if an error is in your favor, as it was with my friend, don't spend the money. It's a crime to steal money from a bank even if they accidentally put it into your account.

Oh, My ACH(ing) Neck

Some years back, every month I would receive a green check in the mail from the Navy Finance Center in Cleveland, Ohio. My military retirement pension. I had to sign it, take it to the bank, deposit it and wait for it to clear before I had access to the funds. Now, however, it is direct deposited; their computer just kisses my bank's computer and the money goes right into my account. Same day. It's great. The biweekly paycheck from my current employer

is also direct deposited.   I also make my monthly car payments and all my insurance payments automatically in
the same way. This reliance on the use of electronic transactions is a widespread and rapidly growing phenomenon
and has serious Y2K implications.
   This technology provides the highest level of convenience, speed and accuracy possible in financial transactions.   It essentially involves just letting the computers
deal directly with one another without human intervention. The process uses a huge computerized system called
the Automated Clearing House (ACH) which is actually a
nationwide network of 38 regional ACH's. The statistics
provided by the National Automated Clearing House Association (NACHA) at their World-WideWeb location are
most revealing.

Transactions: 3.5 billion per year totaling $11 trillion

Participants:

- *500,000 companies*
- *22,000 financial institutions*
- *all 50 state governments*
- *over 1,000 federal agencies*

Transaction types (small sample):

- *payroll*
- *pensions*
- *credit cards*
- *alimony*
- *tax payments*
- *parking fees*

- *dividends*
- *annuities*
- *regular monthly payments*
- *church tithing*
- *government benefits*
- *ATM transactions*

The computer software used by the ACH network is standardized and is provided by the Federal Reserve. This is good news and bad news as far as the Y2K Problem goes. Good news because when centralized, stringent configuration control is used, solving a problem once solves it for everybody. It can be very bad news, however, if the engineers miss something. Then the entire system goes "toes up" as we used to say in the Navy. Complicating the situation is the unfortunate fact that there are still different users at the two ends of the transaction (your employer's bank and your bank, for example) with different computers running different software. Each of which is susceptible to Y2K problems of their own.

Buddy, Can You Loan Me a Dime?

Legend has it that the Y2K Problem was discovered in 1970 by lenders trying to create computerized loan amortization schedules for 30 year real estate loans. The figures for the year 2000 kept coming up incorrect because the software used two digit years. I don't know if this story is true or not, but it certainly does have a certain ring of logic to it. The same error will apply to other interest bearing instruments such as bonds, Certificates of Deposit (CD's), annuities and so on. This flaw could also occur in short-term consumer loan calculations such as those used to figure credit card and charge account interest.

Some really unpleasant results are possible. Lenders, for example, annually send a form to the Internal Revenue Service to report how much interest was paid on home mortgages. This computer generated form could be wildly inaccurate by either too much or too little if the lender's software has a Y2K problem. Another possibility is credit card companies sending bills which claims the borrower owes ninety-nine years worth of interest on the balance of a loan. Of course, that type of errors could work in your favor as well as against it. A bank might, for instance, send a check for 99 years worth of interest on a CD. Again, however, be forewarned. Don't spend the money if your bank makes this sort of error. You can get into trouble even if the error is their fault.

Fortune Tellers

Mankind has always been fascinated with the future. Primitive peoples consult witch doctors, soothsayers and shamans. The religious turn to prayer, scripture, revelation and prophecy. Palm readers, astrologers, tarot card diviners, numerologists and fortune tellers are common even today and television psychics have become tremendously popular. Indeed, dealing with the near future is the central theme of the book you hold in your hand. Our modern civilization has even devised a specialized institution for dealing with the uncertainties of the future. We call it the insurance company. In the following example, I am going to talk mainly about life insurance, but these comments apply to all kinds of insurance including life, health, disability, auto, home, and property.

Insurance companies use mathematical analysis of the past to predict the future. Predicting how long a certain healthy, non-smoking, 30-year old man will live is a pretty tough proposition if you are dealing with one single person. But it becomes much easier if you know how long millions of them have lived in the recent past. Then you can let the numbers work for you and deal with the average, 30-year old man. Although a specific one may die tomorrow, over the long haul, you can predict with stunning accuracy how long the average one will live. Close enough to sell insurance to them and make a profit anyway.

Insurance companies have very high Y2K risk. Since they are an information intensive industry, they are heavily computerized. Virtually all their business activities are done by computer and the most successful companies are those which have automated the most. They use their powerful, mainframe computers to:

- *analyze their mathematical models (called actuarial tables)*

- *maintain massive databases of their customers and policies*

- *process premiums received*

- *process claims received*

- *make payments to valid claimants*

Bad Policy

What kinds of problems might you as a policyholder expect to see as a result of the Y2K situation? The most common is likely to be corruption of their databases which would mean lost or incorrect information. This could result in a multitude of different problems. The first is in the processing of premiums collected. Premiums are, of course the money you or your employer sends to the insurance company every month to pay for the insurance. If these payments are incorrectly processed, premiums which were actually paid on time and in the correct amount might be inaccurately credited to your account or even not credited at all. This could result, of course in the erroneous termination of your policy or the refusal of valid claims or benefits being paid in an incorrect amount.

The second major category is the faulty processing or payment of claims. This type of transaction occurs when you submit paperwork to the insurance company claiming that something bad happened to you such as an accident, or illness requiring a doctor's treatment or perhaps even the death of a loved one. The insurance company validates your claim against your policy and your record of payment and then sends you a check. All of this takes place on their computer system, of course, and Y2K can affect any of these steps along the way to you getting your money.

Oh, yes. One additional thing. It is obvious, but worth mentioning anyway. When either you pay the insurance company its premiums or when they pay you your claim, the transaction is typically done by check. involving at least a couple of banks in the transaction. As you will remember from the section above, that introduces another Y2K land mine along the way.

Big Money

The second serious danger to insurance owners would be the collapse of the insurance company due to investment losses. This would result, of course, in the loss to you of all premiums paid and all cash value accumulated and would leave you without insurance coverage. The insurance industry has total annual income of about $800 billion, a staggering amount. What in the world do they do with it all? Well, some is paid out in claims of course and some is used for operating expenses and some, of course, is profit. They also have to keep a lot of it in reserve and ready to pay all those policy holders at some time in the future. So they do what you might expect, they invest it. And this is their second big Y2K risk.

Along with corporate pensions, insurance companies are among the largest of the "institutional investors." As this is written (late 1996), their investment portfolio exceeds $3 trillion (3,000,000,000,000 dollars!) and, according to the Statistical Abstract of the United States, consists of about:

- *$0.2 trillion in government securities*

- *$1.2 trillion in real estate and mortgages*

- *$1.6 trillion in stocks, bonds, mutual funds*

This last chunk is what creates such a monstrous Y2K problem. The investment industry and the insurance industry are like two economic giants locked into a tight embrace and dancing the night away. If one of them stumbles, they will both fall down in the middle of the dance floor. They are so tightly connected together that if Y2K causes problems on the stock market, the insurance companies will suffer. Likewise, if the insurance industry staggers, the investment world will stumble too.

In All Fairness

Let me be fair to the insurance industry here and mention that of all the industries in the country, they were among the first to foresee the implications of the Y2K crisis and the first to get started in fixing the problem. Being naturally concerned for my own hide, I checked with my own insurance company, United Services Automobile Association (USAA) and found that they started working on the problem in 1989. Their approach to the problem was to set up a total duplicate set of computer software and then rebuild or repair the entire system one piece at a time. They started with small pieces to help them get smart before taking on the huge policies. (The first element they fixed consisted of cruise ship vacation policies.) USAA plans to be finished before the end of 1998 which will give them all of 1999 to conduct full scale testing. Another good example is the Prudential Life Insurance Company. They currently have <u>six hundred</u> full time computer programmers working on the problem. They plan to spend about <u>one hundred twenty million dollars</u> to fix their problem. They also project that they will be finished before the end of 1998.

Now, before you get all misty eyed with relief, consider this. After several years of extraordinary effort and at a breathtaking cost, these two companies are talking about getting done <u>just in time</u>. Keep in mind, in life insurance alone there are over 2000 companies in the United States. Many of these just plain don't have the technical savvy to do what needs to be done. Others will not be able to afford spending the huge amounts of money required to fix the problem. Still others will get started too late and will run out of time. In fact, there is little chance indeed that all of them will be ready in time. Here is a quote from an engineer who works a lot with the AS/400 computer made by IBM. There are about a third of a million of these midsize computers in use, many of them by small and medium businesses including insurance companies.

> In short, if you are on a midrange platform with date-dependent applications and can't replace your existing systems with new compliant (software) packages, start thinking about bankruptcy now..

I certainly don't claim that this gentleman speaks for all computer engineers, but I can say from experience that many, many of them feel exactly this way.

Just Plain Bill

If there is a single piece of the Y2K Crisis I feel confident in making predictions about it is this one. I can virtually guarantee you will receive incorrect, computer-generated bills in the mail due to Y2K foul-ups. It will mainly be an inconvenience for consumers but it will likely drive some companies right out of business. Many business concerns operate fairly close to the edge when it comes to cash flow. Many of these, such as utilities, banks, credit card companies, department stores, and insurance companies. send out bills on a monthly basis and simply can't survive even a one month interruption in cash flow.

Interestingly, the larger the ratio of faulty transactions they experience, the better it will be for you. I know that sounds funny but hear me out. Suppose your local cable-TV company has a serious Y2K problem in their billing software resulting in incorrect billings for half their customers. A problem of that magnitude will draw lots of public attention and will end up on the local evening television news. In these circumstances, the company president and the local media are all going to be on your side in trying to solve the problem. Imagine, however, that just one customer in a thousand (including you) gets a grossly faulty bill. Now you will either have to pay up and then fight back or refuse to pay and get your service turned off while the fight takes place. This is the type of billing problem to be very alert for. If you do receive a seriously inaccurate bill, don't contact the company that sent it for a couple of days. Instead, check out the local news to see if the problem is widespread. If so, there will be instructions given on TV and radio or in the papers on how to handle the situation. If the media make no mention of widespread problems I know of no other recourse but to seek legal help.

Action Steps

Spike Date Precautions.

By now, these Spike Date precautions should be start-ing to come pretty naturally to you. An obvious Spike Date precaution is just simply to be aware. Be wary of Spike Dates and their potential for harm. Pay attention to your local news on radio, TV and in the local newspapers. Watch for failures or unexplained disruptions in service in financial institutions such as banks, credit unions and S&L's. Be ready to respond quickly to withdraw your funds if necessary.

Investment activities of all types should be avoided if at possible on and around Spike Dates. Do not purchase, trade, transfer, convert or sell investments that are pro-cessed in any way by computers. This includes all stock market transactions, of course including transactions through either a stockbroker or a mutual fund manager. This precaution extends to IRA accounts and 401(k) ac-counts as well as regular investments. Also do not open or close stock trading accounts or mutual fund accounts on or around Spike Dates.

Banking transactions of all kinds should be avoided close to Spike Dates. Don't make deposits or withdrawals, write checks, use credit cards or debit cards, use Automatic Teller Machines or do any banking by mail, telephone or personal computer. Limit yourself to cash transactions at least for a few days before and after Spike Dates. Also don't open, close or liquidate bank accounts.

Don't make any major purchases, sales or transfers (even if you use all cash) on or around Spike Dates. Real estate purchases, for example, are recorded at the court house on computers. These transactions have serious le-gal and taxation consequences and should be avoided on these critical dates. Automobile transactions also have serious legal ramifications in that transactions must be registered with the local authorities. Believe me, as badly as most state departments of motor vehicles can screw things up under normal circumstances, don't subject yourself to all that mess topped off by some sort of Y2K difficulty with the states' computer systems.

All banks, credit/debit/charge card companies and investment managers issue periodic statements (typically monthly) of your account history. The first statement you receive following any Spike Date should be examined with the greatest care. Look for anything unusual and immediately get into contact with the source of the statement if there is any kind of irregularity. This will likely be a frustrating experience because you will typically be dealing, on the first call at least, with a junior clerk of some sort. BE RELENTLESS. Demand to talk to a supervisor. When you get that person on the phone, demand to talk to his or her supervisor. Keep at it until you get someone in real authority.

Another step you might take is to record the conversation. For $30-40 at Radio Shack you can purchase an inexpensive but very serviceable small tape recorder with a suction cup microphone which sticks right onto the telephone. (An important point- you must inform the other party you are recording the conversation because it is illegal to record without both parties consent.) This will be a powerful tool, however, when dealing with a snotty clerk. Ask for the clerk's full name and tell them to speak slowly and clearly so your lawyer will be able to understand the tape. That ought to get their attention quickly and should get a supervisor to the phone in a hurry as well.

Insurance companies, on the other hand, often do not issue periodic statements so it would be a prudent idea to call them just after Spike Dates to verify receipt and proper posting of your premium payment. It would also be a good idea to record these conversations.

If you have money automatically deposited in or withdrawn from your bank account, you must be especially diligent around Spike Dates. Don't wait until statement time to verify that the transaction has been properly posted. Call your banking institution to be certain.

Continuing Precautions.

There are a wide range of precautions to be taken on a regular basis concerning your financial matters. The first of these deals with investment matters. What kinds of companies should you invest in from now until after the Year 2000 Problem has subsided? And what kind you should avoid? This is a tough call because I am in no way an investment expert. I guess, in general, I would cast a suspicious eye on high tech companies who sell computer equipment or software. I would also shy away from companies whose main business activity involves the production of intangible goods and revolves entirely around the use of computers and software such as insurance companies and the financial sector. In my judgment, these kinds of companies stand the highest risk of being impacted by Y2K.

Company size is also a determining factor in Y2K investment risk. The larger the company, the more and better the resources they are likely to have to apply to their Y2K problem. Very small companies on the other hand are probably less dependent on very large computer systems. They are more likely to use off-the-shelf software and common, personal computers which are somewhat easier to cure of Y2K-itis than the larger systems used by the bigger companies. The mid-size companies will be the ones to avoid from an investment standpoint. They are both dependent on larger systems and less likely to have the resources to solve the problem. Many analysts predict that midsize businesses will suffer the most from Y2K and are at the greatest risk of failure.

It might appear on the surface there would be a great stock play in companies that specialize in solving Y2K problems. I am fairly close to this situation in my employment role and I can tell you that there are plenty of snake oil salesmen coming onto the Y2K scene. As the crisis deepens and more companies become aware of the serious nature of their problem, more of these shysters will come crawling out of the woodwork. My guess is this will be a very volatile market segment. Another factor is these companies will put themselves at significant risk for Y2K lawsuits from clients who use them but still fail to clear up their Y2K problems. Suing Y2K repair companies will be a cottage industry all its own.

Another factor is these Y2K specialists are going to be legally liable for their work. Many companies are not going to be ready for the Y2K Crisis. As we get into late 1998 and onwards, the Y2K specialty companies will increasingly be the target of lawsuits from these failed and about-to-fail outfits. In general, therefore, I just think the "Y2K Fixer" companies are investments which carry significant risk and I would avoid them.

So who might weather the Y2K storm better than most? Well, I might feel a little warm and fuzzy toward companies who dealt in the production of tangible goods and companies involved in natural resources such as agriculture, mining and timber. Service companies might also seem more attractive by the same thinking. Y2K won't have any effect on the ore in a mine or the trees on a mountainside. Likewise, businesses which are based on the services provided by a group of highly talented people may be less threatened by Y2K than others. Those talents will, after all, still be there when the year 2000 rolls around.

For investment purposes, I guess I would also lean toward companies whose products and services are deemed to be Y2K Compliant. These will be the "early adopters" of Y2K. In other words, they are the companies who recognized early on the nature of the problem and then applied themselves to solving the problem while there was time to accomplish the repairs in a timely and orderly fashion.

The real problem with leaving your money in the stock market, of course, is not deciding what stocks to invest in. It is the fact that the marketplace itself could collapse or experience terrible disruptions due to Y2K-related problems in the vast computer systems used to operate the market. (One stock exchange, the NASDAQ, consists entirely of computers.) Of course, another investment option is available and this is one which shields your assets from Y2K completely - getting out of the stock market altogether. This is what I recommend because it is the very safest thing you can do.

I think the economic situation and, specifically, the stock market problems caused by Y2K will be severe enough to justify this action. No, I am not predicting a stock market collapse, although there is a real possibility of this happening. There IS a strong possibility of serious disruptions, however, and I think it is prudent to avoid the potential harm from those disruptions.

My belief is your fundamental strategy for the next several years should be safety. You have several options if you decide to take this approach. The first is to invest in hard assets only such as gold, silver, gemstones, or real estate. You could also convert directly to cash. Finally, you can convert to US Treasury instruments (bonds, bills or notes) which will at least pull in some interest. If you do this, take possession of the instruments themselves. Don't leave them in the hands of your stockbroker and his computer system.

Most people believe if your assets are tied up in tax deferred investments such as IRA or 401(k) plans you can't make some of these kinds of investments, but that is not true. Your options are indeed slightly limited (no collectibles, antiques, art work, etc.) but U.S. gold and silver coins (one ounce or less are allowed) and you can invest in most other hard assets including real estate using your tax deferred investment vehicles. You just can't use the investments for your own purposes which means you can't buy a house and live in it, buy furniture or art work for your house, etc. Talk to the trust department of your bank or your tax person; better yet get a copy of IRS Publication 590 <u>Individual Retirement Accounts</u> (IRA s), which covers this point.

If you decide to pull out of the stock market, when should you make the big move? I personally will be out before the first big Spike Date which is July 1, 1998. That will provide the maximum security. I would certainly delay no longer than December 31, 1998.

A strong suggestion I have in dealing with financial institutions is to beat them to death with letters. Chapter 11 of this Survival Guide is devoted to just this topic. It provides guidance in how to use the power of the pen to sway public officials as well as board members and officers of corporations in the way they are addressing the Y2K issue. Additionally, Appendix B provides sample letters just for this purpose.

I also suggest that you sit down at the end of a month and review all the bills you pay and ask yourself this question, "What happens to me and my family if the company that receives this payment goes under or stops providing me with their services?" Make up a list of the failures that would be most damaging to you and start protecting yourself against those problems first.

Don't keep any more money in the bank than you can afford to lose or to have tied for up for some period of time. Nobody likes to lose any money, of course, but just remember, if it's in the bank, you are at risk. All I suggest is that you use risk management techniques. Keep a cash reserve set aside which is sufficient to cover your bills for several months just as insurance. Then don't use the banks anymore than is necessary. If your checking account draws some interest, and you stand to lose a little money by keeping your account to a minimum, I wouldn't let that bother me. It is better by far to lose out on a little interest than to lose all the principle you have on deposit. Of course, you might not lose the money at all, you just might not be able to get access to it quickly due to disruptions in banking service.

Remember, the risk of a total banking collapse is very high. My guess is fifty-fifty at least. Consider how to arrange your affairs so you can survive in a world without banks for a while. Weeks or months at a minimum.

Keep your eyes open for products and companies that claim Y2K compliance. Try to use these companies and their products. First you will be rewarding companies which have solved their Y2K problem. You are secondarily punishing companies who are not taking care of their Y2K problem by withholding your business from them.

"Yesterday, all my troubles seemed so far away.
Now it looks as though they're here to stay."

"Yesterday" - the Beatles

Chapter 7

Y2K And Your
Vital Information

Imagine

There is a recent movie thriller titled <u>The Net</u>, starring
Sandra Bullock in which the main character's identity is
stolen from her when the bad guys somehow use the Internet to remove her important personal information
from all the databases in the world. Sort of like a one person, Y2K nightmare. The Year 2000 computer crisis, however, won't be limited to just one pretty girl in a movie. It
will be a nightmare for the whole world. Close your eyes
for a moment and imagine what might happen to you,
your family and friends when <u>your</u> vital information
becomes altered or destroyed.

Your nephew Frank recently decided to apply for
graduate school so he requested   transcripts from his
alma mater. Last week he received a letter from the
school stating that his name doesn't appear in their
records as having attended that university. He is now
frantically searching the boxes in his attic for his old

grade reports..

A few days later, you receive a letter from the government claiming that you are overdue in paying on your student loan. With back interest, they claim you now owe more than $100,000. You paid the loan off twelve years ago but you have moved since then and can't find the paperwork.

This is disastrous since you are about to apply for a mortgage to buy your dream house. Fearful that the false information will show up in your credit history, you send a request to all three of the main credit reporting bureaus asking for copies of your credit report. Then the really bad news arrives. All three reports show that one of your credit cards hasn't been paid for two years. They indicate you owe $15,000. You are, of course, completely up to date on all your credit cards.

Your nephew Frank's problems mount when he receives notice from the Selective Service that he is in violation of the law because he has not registered for the draft. Frank, who is twenty-seven, registered the day after his eighteenth birthday.

I could drag this out for several pages but this is enough for you to start getting the picture.

Information Please

Vital information about you resides in computers all across the land and every one of them is susceptible to the Year 2000 Computer Problem. This chapter is about your personal, vital information and what can happen when the Y2K Crisis gets up close and personal. Some of this vital information is in the hands of government agencies. Some is maintained by private business concerns such as merchants, mailing lists and credit reporting bureaus.

Other information is kept by institutions such as schools, universities, libraries, hospitals and charitable organizations. As discussed earlier, Y2K is essentially an information corruption problem. To protect your vital information you should know where it resides and how that information might become corrupted because of Y2K. You also need to know specific actions you can take to protect yourself. First we will take a look at some of the federal government databases that are crucial to your well being.

Social Insecurity Revisited

For every hundred dollars in earnings you make (wages, salary, bonuses, commissions, tips, etc.), about $15 gets paid to your Social Security account. You pay half that amount out of your paycheck and your employer pays the other half. You have paid into this account all your working life. Imagine your account is a coffee can with your name on it. Every month your employer sends that fifteen bucks to Uncle Sam, the keeper of the can. Many people believe Uncle Sam puts your money into your coffee can to keep it safe for your retirement, but this is not the case. He spends every single dime like a drunken sailor (boy, it pains me to say that). The only thing that goes into the can is a receipt for the amount you paid. For all those years, that is the only thing that has been put into the can. When your retirement comes along, Uncle Sam gets your receipts out of the can, adds up how much you have put in and uses a set formula to determine what your monthly Social Security benefits will be.

Now imagine that Uncle Sam gets into your can and discovers that your receipts are gone. Or, they been damaged and are unreadable. He no longer knows whether or not you are eligible for benefits or what the correct amount is. That's what will happen if the Social Security

Administration (SSA) doesn't get their Y2K Problem fixed in time. (I indicated in the chapter on the federal government how they were doing. Six months after they announced that the project required 100 computer programmers for three years, they increased their staffing estimate by sixty percent. Not a good sign to be sure.)

The Social Security program has been in effect for more than sixty years. All the people who have ever worked in the United States during that entire time are in the SSA databases. Including you. Those databases and the computer programs that use them could be seriously damaged by the Y2K Computer Problem. The problem could be slight or it could be disastrous. Considering the general effectiveness of the government across the board, I strongly advise that steps be taken by everyone who could be affected by problems in those databases to protect themselves.

The first step is to obtain a Statement of Earnings and Benefits from the Social Security Administration. Call their national toll free number at 1-800-772-1213 and ask them to send you SSA Form 7004. This phone number gets a lot of business so, if you can't get through, try their Office of Public Inquiries in Baltimore, Maryland, at 410-965-7700 or look in your local telephone book for the nearest SSA office. Complete and submit the form and in about six weeks you'll receive your statement in the mail. Be sure to keep the cover letter that comes back with the statement. Remember, you are preserving this information to help prove your case in the event of future disputes with the Social Security Administration. Another alternative is to enlist the help of a life insurance agent. They often have these forms. If yours doesn't, call a few different insurance companies around town. I bet they'll fall all over themselves to provide this service for free in the hopes of gaining a client.

The next step is to keep doing the first step. Every six months, order another Statement of Earnings and Benefits. Build up a portfolio of these documents. There won't be big differences between copies that have just six months between versions, but the exact figures are not what is important. Remember, what you are doing is building up a sequence of documents which are consistent with one another and show your account over time. If you start now and continue until after Y2K has played itself out, you will be able to deal with the Social Security Administration from a position of real strength if troubles do come up.

This goes back to one of my primary Y2K prescriptive measures and that is to build a Y2K Shield by becoming your own librarian. It is critical that you take charge of your vital information by managing it effectively and thereby protecting it from the data corruption that is coming from Y2K.

If you are currently receiving Social Security checks, there is one additional step you should take. Keep a copy of your checks in your Vital Information Portfolio. If they are direct deposited, keep a copy of your bank statements and the deposit slip you receive in the mail. You will need to have as big a collection of this kind of paper as you can accumulate. I know it seems like a hassle. It is a hassle, but it may save you from serious difficulties at some point down the road when the Y2K gremlins are stalking the land.

All That You Could Be

If you have served in the military, there are a couple of special vital information considerations for you. Anyone who was on active duty long enough (different terms for different programs) is classified as a veteran and is eligible for a multitude of veteran's benefits. Several of the most widely used of these benefits are:

- *no money down home loans guaranteed by the Veteran's Administration (VA)*

- *GI Bill payment for college or training expenses*

- *treatment at VA medical facilities for service connected medical conditions*

- *burial in national cemeteries*

The VA maintains your records (and millions of others) in computerized databases which are candidates for corruption as the Y2K problem progresses. Probably, the most serious effect would be erroneous denial of benefits to those who legitimately qualify for them. This could prevent you from getting a VA loan for example or stop you from obtaining medical care in a VA medical facility.

As with most of these vitally important databases, your first line of defense against Y2K problems is to attempt to obtain a hard copy of the data. There is one general and critical piece of documentation you must have to prove your military service and that is the DD Form 214 "Statement of Military Service." If you are a veteran, you were given this form when you were discharged from the service. To obtain a copy of this vital form or any part of your military service or medical records, contact the following:

National Personnel Records Center
9700 Page Boulevard
St. Louis MO 63132-5200

They require a written request and you must provide them with your full name, address, Social Security number, service number, branch of service, all dates of service, and date and place of birth.

To verify eligibility for a VA loan, a specific form is required. It is called, creatively, a "Request for Determination of Eligibility and Available Loan Guaranty Entitlement," which is VA Form 26-1880. You can obtain one easily at any real estate broker's office. Keep a copy of the completed form, send it in along with a copy of your DD 214 and then add the resulting documentation to your Vital Information portfolio. I recommend you go through this procedure even if you are not interested in obtaining a real estate loan because having the paperwork in your portfolio will strengthen your case in the event of any confrontation with the Veteran's Administration over your eligibility for any other benefits.

GI Bill

If you were on active service after 1984 you may have participated in the Montgomery GI Bill program wherein your contributions were matched by the service during your tenure. On separation, you can draw from your account to help defray expenses of college or an approved training course. The Veteran's Administration manages these accounts in a computerized database which is susceptible, of course, to Y2K difficulties. These difficulties could result in the inaccurate posting of information to your account or in the loss of information altogether. If you are attending school and receiving payments, keep a copy of everything you receive including the checks themselves and any statements that are forwarded. You can track the status of your account by contacting the VA at 1-800-827-1000. Give them your Social Security number and name and they will provide you with your account information. Be sure to ask for a hard copy so you can add it to your vital information portfolio.

Drafted

All male citizens are required by law to register for the draft with the Selective Service within a year of their eighteenth birthday. Even though the military services are not currently manned by this method, the requirement is kept on the books in the event of a national emergency. The accuracy of your Selective Service records is important to you for two reasons. You obviously don't want to be erroneously drafted even in the event of a national emergency. Additionally, you don't want the federal government incorrectly believing you are in violation of the law. You can obtain your Selective Service registration status by requesting it in writing from:

U.S. Selective Service
Registration Information Office
PO Box 4368
North Suburban IL 60197-4638

The telephone number for this office is 708-688-6888

Miscellaneous

There are many other federal databases which could be vital to you but I can't be all-inclusive here. Again, I strongly suggest you obtain a copy of Lesko's <u>Info-Power III</u> and just spend a few evenings going through it. It offers over 15,000 sources of information available at all levels of government as well as commercial sources. Just reading it will probably remind you of what is important for you to have and it will show you how to get it as well.

Freedom Of Information Act

There are important legal ramifications to obtaining information held by the federal government. The law is clear on this issue as is indicated by its name - the Freedom of Information Act (FOIA). Basically, unless the information is classified, meaning it is protected for national security reasons, you have the legal right to obtain the information. All that is required is that you make a proper written request to the federal agency that keeps the information you want. You also need to clearly identify to that agency what information you want. This is done with a pretty straightforward letter. Appendix B has a sample for you to use. In my work as a government contractor in the past, I have exercised this procedure several times and am happy to report that, in every instance, my request was handled rapidly and efficiently. You will sometimes be required to pay a nominal fee for the reproduction costs but overall the process works pretty effectively.

Federal Retirement

If you are retired as a result of federal service, whether military or Civil Service, there are additional factors involved in protecting your vital data. Your retirement check is drawn on the US Treasury and made out by a finance center which maintains your data in their computerized database. You can best protect yourself by keeping a copy of the documentation that is sent to you around the end of the tax year. Each year, as a retired Navy man, I receive two documents. In December, I receive notification of the cost of living increase I can expect to see when the new year starts. Then, after the year is finished, I receive a tax form showing how much I was paid and how much was withheld from my pay for income tax purposes. You should keep each of these forms and add them to your portfolio. You probably have a copy of the tax form if you have a copy of your tax return. To obtain a copy of your financial records themselves contact the agency that sends you your monthly checks or the two annual statements.

Infernal Revenue

For certain. You know what could happen here and the answer is simple. Get copies of your complete tax returns for the past five years by filing IRS Form 4506, Request for Copy of Tax Form, with the IRS center which processes your tax return. The charge for each return is $14. I recommend that you order these copies <u>even if you kept copies of the returns yourself</u>. Keep the copies provided with a copy of the Form 4506 and the letter the IRS sends with your returns. Remember, the purpose of all this drill is to establish a hard copy of the data the IRS has, not what you kept several years ago. You are collecting ammunition to use in the event there is a dispute resulting from Y2K problems in the future. Keep your Vital Information portfolio up to date by retaining copies of all tax returns you submit between now and the year 2005 at least. The recommendations in this paragraph are very important. The Internal Revenue Service is a tremendously weak link in the federal system from a computer aspect. I am convinced they are going to have serious Y2K problems.

Student Loans

Because student loan programs are so prevalent they deserve a brief mention here. If you have ever had one in the past, there is a computerized record of your loan account in the Department of Education. Corruption of these loan records could lead to several different kinds of problems as a result of the Y2K Crisis. Examples are inaccurate accounting of payments made, posting of your loan payments to the wrong account, the false reactivation of paid-in-full accounts or even the accidental deletion of your record. You can obtain a copy of the records of payment by contacting:

Loan Records Office
Student Financial Assistance Programs
Office of Post Secondary Education
US Department of Education
600 Independence Ave., S.W.
Washington ,DC 20202

You can also obtain your records by telephone at 202-708-9448. The only information needed is your name, address and Social Security number.

The above provides information on some of the most important types of federal government databases which contain information vital to your well-being. There are many others, of course, but it has been the intent here to cover the most common. When designing your vital information portfolio, you would be well advised to reflect back on your affairs to determine other databases which could be important to you and then try to obtain a hard copy of your records. As mentioned earlier, Matthew Lesko's book, Info-Power III, is a great place to start in tracking down the source of this information. Let us now move on to the other governmental repositories of your vital information - the state you live in.

Mirror Image

By and large, the states maintain a number of databases which are largely equivalent to federal databases and your action should be a mirror image as well. Two examples are getting copies of your state income tax returns and state sponsored student loan records. Follow the same steps to acquire the same information from the appropriate state agencies. Lesko's book can again give you a great head start here.

You, You're Driving Me Crazy

Your state probably maintains at least three databases concerning you and your automobile that are important elements of your vital information base. The first contains driver's license record information and the Y2K problem is alive and well here because licenses are already being issued which expire in the year 2000. For example, some driver's licenses are being rejected by rental car agencies today because their expiration year reads "00." If your card expires in this year, it is a probable source of trouble to you now as well as in the future. Try very hard to replace it with one that expires in a different year. Try growing a beard, shaving your head, getting married, changing your name, moving to a new address or smearing the darn thing with fish oil so the cat will eat it. Whatever it might take to qualify for a new license. By all means don't tell them you want a new license because you are concerned about the Y2K Problem. They'll turn you down for certain.

Driving records will be also become corrupted. This will have a very bad effect on automobile insurance rates and coverages because these insurance companies use these driving records extensively to determine eligibility for and cost of automobile insurance. Since these records are kept by the states it means there are 50 different sources of Y2K problems. I believe they will indeed be a major problem if just a few states have problems, it will be a major difficulty for all auto insurance companies doing business in those few states.

Finally automobile registration records will also develop Y2K problems. Since most families these days own two or even more automobiles, this multiplies the possibilities of Y2K problems for each family, of course.

Data corruption in the driver's license and auto registration databases could give you problems with law enforcement officers. Getting pulled over for a burnt out taillight could lead to a most unpleasant adventure if a police officer is given incorrect information on you and your driving related information.

Your driver's license and auto registration are documents you physically keep on hand, usually in your automobile and wallet. This is legally required in most states, of course. You have probably never even seen a copy of your driving record, however. To protect yourself, I suggest that you obtain a copy of each record from your state's Department of Motor Vehicles or whatever the agency is called in your state. These are personal records and the state cannot withhold them from you. The address of your favorite agency can be found in your local telephone book or in Lesko's Info-Power III.

May I See Your License, Please

Many occupations require licenses above and beyond a simple business license. Some examples are:

Doctor	*Lawyer*
Dentist	*Realtor*

Barber   Social Worker
Hearing Aid Dealer   Precious Metals Dealer
Day Care Operator   Nursing Home Operator
Security Guard   Veterinarian
Insurance Agent   Architect
Plumber   Cosmetologist

and so on. Notice that many of the above such as doctor, lawyer and architect are what are typically referred to as the "professions," but many are not.

If you are employed in one of these occupations or in any occupation requiring a special license, contact your state licensing board and get a copy of your records. Lesko's Info-Power III has a complete state by state listing of these offices. Just having a copy of your license itself is not satisfactory. Send them a letter (keeping a copy, of course) and put the response and the copy of your records into your portfolio.

There are other state maintained databases which could be important to you but those mentioned above are some of the most important. Let us now now move on to the data that is maintained by the lowest level of government - your city and/or county.

Localized Pain

Your local government maintains some extremely important databases that are critically important to you. As discussed earlier in this Survival Guide, these databases will be very susceptible to the Y2K problem for many reasons. Accordingly, you should be especially diligent in protecting yourself against these problems. Happily, since these agencies are right in your community, there is a good chance you can see your information and get good hard copies of it without too much difficulty.

The Landed Gentry

Some of the most important databases maintained by your local government are real estate records. Two types of these are paramount, transaction records and tax records. Real estate transaction records are those which are recorded by your lawyer when you buy, sell, or transfer property. They include such things as deeds, deeds of trust, mortgages, land contracts, leases, options, mortgage releases, PLATS and so on. Typically these documents are maintained as reproduced images kept in massive sets of bound volumes. Since this information is maintained as reproduced images how can this data be jeopardized by the Y2K computer crisis? The answer is that the books themselves will be unaffected but the computerized listings of what is kept in the books could become corrupted. If this happens, your data would still be good but you wouldn't know which book to find it in. The solution to this kind of problem is to keep copies of the information yourself but also to go to the courthouse and get a copy of the computer printout that tells which books your data is located in. If this task is something you don't wish to take on, speak to your real estate lawyer or to a title company. They would be happy to get the information for you for a modest fee.

You should also get a hard copy of your property tax records. Most property taxes are paid as part of your mortgage payment and the bills and receipts are sent to your lender rather than you so you will have to put in a little work to get this information. Fortunately, this is a fairly easy undertaking. Each county typically has a Tax Assessment Office (or something similarly named). It is often at or close to the county courthouse. Visit this office and just request the clerk to make you a copy of all your tax records for the past five years. If there is a cost for this service, it should be nominal. It would be a good idea to have these documents dated and stamped certified or original to verify their official status. I recommend you obtain these hard copies even if you have past records on hand. Both sets could be required later to help you in the event of disputes.

Vital Statistics

Government mandates the collection of data on some important personal social transactions and some of this data is even called "vital statistics." Here is a partial list of these transactions:

Marriage	*Divorce*
Birth	*Death*
Adoption	*Name Change*
Judgment	*Collateralized Debt*
Business License	*Business Name*

Data concerning these important social transactions are typically maintained at a county courthouse. The primary way to protect this information, of course, is to simply be certain that you have a copy of the documents involved. Like real estate records (which also fit into this category but which have already been discussed) these records are often maintained as reproduced images in large bound volumes. The index used to locate the data is computerized, however, making the location information susceptible to Y2K problems. (It should be mentioned that bankruptcy also falls into this category but is a federally managed transaction which is found only at federal courthouses.) If you have been bankrupt, be certain to remember to go to the federal courthouse where the case was adjudicated and get a copy of the paperwork.

School Daze I

All public school records are in jeopardy from the Y2K computer crisis. By and large, public school technical support staffs are frequently inadequate in number and in programming expertise. The chance that they will know about and be able to cure the Y2K problems with their computers is very slim indeed. The records could be either corrupted or lost altogether. This could affect high school age children more seriously as it could have an impact on their ability to obtain employment, enter the armed forces or gain admission to the college of their choice. Accordingly, visit your childrens' schools and obtain a printout of their entire academic file. At the conclusion of each year repeat this process and each academic term be certain to add report cards to the collection. In general, the older the child, the more important the records. It also becomes more important if your family moves a lot because your ability to deal with out of state schools will be more difficult.

Get Out The Vote

In another chapter, I discuss the potential implications of Y2K on elections. For you as an individual, Y2K problems in voter registration records could prevent you from voting. Accordingly, I suggest that you visit your local election officials and request a copy of the computer printout that contains your registration information. Have them date and stamp the information for official verification and add it to your vital information portfolio.

Medical Records

Medical records are probably your most vital institutional information. These could reside at the federal level if you are being treated (or have been treated) at a federally operated medical facility such as those operated by the military, the Public Health Service or the Veteran's Administration. These kinds of records could also be maintained by your local hospital or medical center. It is important to note that the records themselves are of <u>three</u> important and very different types.

The first of these is the actual medical records which keep track of your actual medical condition and the treatments and medications you have received. These are critical, of course, because your past condition and treatment are often important factors in any current or future treatment you may have to undergo. In other words, the medical art is highly dependent on your medical history. Y2K has the potential to corrupt or even destroy your computerized medical history data. This could obviously result in mistakes, even fatal mistakes, being made in your medical treatment.

It is highly likely that Y2K will kill people. One of the greatest possibilities is these deaths will occur because of errors in patient databases which become contaminated due to the Y2K problem. Improper medicines may be dispensed, inaccurate amounts of prescription medicines could be administered and patients whose age is critical to their proper treatment (such as the elderly and the very young) will be incorrectly treated because computer databases might miscalculate patient ages.

The second type of medical record that is important is that which deals with your medical insurance. For discussion purposes here I include commercial medical insurance such as that provided as a fringe benefit by most employers as well as Medicare, Medicaid, CHAMPUS, TRICARE and all other government-provided health benefit programs. This part of your medical record deals with who pays for the treatment whatever the source.

Problems in this part of your medical record may not be potentially dangerous but could certainly be a major inconvenience because you could mistakenly be denied insurance coverage due to errors in this data. If you are seriously ill or injured, treatment will certainly be provided no matter how you are covered, but for non-life threatening illnesses you might have to do battle with the hospital or with your insurance provider to prove your coverage.

The third important type of medical record which could might become unreliable due to Y2K is your record of payments made for treatment. Most types of medical insurance, even some of the government provided programs, involve some sort of deductible or co-payment. You might have to pay just $5 per visit or up to 50% of the total bill for some kinds of plans. Problems in this database would not be threatening to your health but could certainly challenge you financially.

The primary set of strategies used to protect your vital information is: a) get copies of your data and b) keep all information that comes to you. Quite frankly, in the case of medical records, I believe you will have modest if any success at prying your data out of the hands of the medical and insurance establishments. This does not mean you should not make the attempt. You should be forewarned, however, that your chances of success are slim.

Here is what I suggest to improve your chances. Do a little research and identify the senior official involved such as the Chairman of the Board or President of your local hospital for example. Enlist the aid of a reference librarian at your local library for this information. Then write this person a brief but forceful request for your records. Be sure to ask for all three types of records; medical, medical insurance and financial. Now here is the key to using this approach. Don't send the letter the regular way. Instead, send it Certified - Return Receipt Requested. This means the official (or actually his secretary or administrative aide) has to sign a receipt for the letter and the post office then sends the receipt back to you, with the signature on it. It is the same letter, but you are sending a signal to the recipient you are serious in making the request. Another technique which can be used which is stronger yet is to have the letter sent by your lawyer. This will cost you a few bucks but might get you some serious attention.

The other main thing you should do, of course, is to start keeping a copy of everything having to do with your medical situation. This should make up a separate part of your vital information portfolio and should include bills, prescriptions, correspondence with your insurance provider etc. When the full fury of the Y2K storm hits, this could end up being the most critical single chunk of your personally vital information bank.

School Daze II

The other set of school records which are in Y2K jeopardy are those maintained by institutions of higher learning. Next year I will have three of my children attending college so I can attest to the sacrifice and expense involved in acquiring education for one's grown children. I can imagine very little that would be more personally devastating than to have their academic records contaminated or lost. If you or anyone in your family is currently a college student, obtain annual copies of transcripts and retain all term grade reports. Be sure the transcripts are certified with a raised seal. These documents will cost about six dollars or so apiece but if your pride and joy is attending a $25,000 per year premium university, that six bucks could end up being a terrific investment. Incidentally, colleges will experience their own "specialty spike date" with students who will be in the graduating class of "00."

If you do not have family members currently enrolled in college but do have college graduates in the family, you should go ahead now and obtain backup copies of their transcripts for your vital information portfolio. These can be obtained by contacting the Registrar at your college.

Bills, Bills, Bills

In an earlier chapter in which I discussed the financial implications of the Year 2000 Crisis, I boldly predicted that you would experience problems with the receipt of inaccurate billings from providers of goods and services such as merchants and utilities. Problems with your data in these databases could result in financial damage as well as the loss or interruption of the good or service. The solution is simple. Keep copies. Keep copies. Keep copies.

Credit Records

There isn't much in the way of fouled up databases that will cause you more grief than a faulty credit report. Unhappily, the credit reporting industry is a sitting duck for the Y2K gun. An inaccurate credit report could prevent you from obtaining credit such as credit cards and home mortgages. This might not be such a big deal except the credit reporting companies have a terrible reputation for their very poor performance in correcting errors in their databases. Any credit reporting company which has not perfectly cleansed its databases and computer software of Y2K contamination, will be absolutely flooded with demands from irate clients with corrupted data. The effects will be overwhelming and you need to be very diligent in protecting yourself from Y2K problems in this arena.

The solution is to collect a <u>sequence</u> of credit reports from each company in your vital information portfolio. I suggest one every six months from now until a couple of years past the year 2000. Having several sequential reports will be critical when and if your information suddenly changes due to some Y2K error in the data.

There are three major credit reporting bureaus and many smaller, regional ones. You can locate these smaller companies in the yellow pages under the heading "Credit Reporting Agencies." Information on the three major companies is provided below.

Typically, you can obtain one report yearly at no cost with a small charge for additional reports. You need to include your name, address, social security #, and your Birthdate, along with prior addresses for the past five years and other names (like a maiden name) you have been known by in that 5 year period. You should include a copy of your driver's license (if it shows your current home address - if it doesn't, you'll need to send a copy of a utility bill) You'll also need to include a copy of your Social Security Card. If you don't have one, a medical insurance card with the policy number, a W2 form, tax return or bank statement will do.

The three major credit reporting bureaus can be contacted at the following:

Trans Union
760 Sproul Road
Springfield PA 19064

Experian Nat'l Consumer Assistance Ctr
P.O. Box 949
Allen, TX 75013-0949

Equifax Credit Information Services
PO Box 740256
Atlanta GA 30374

When you receive your credit information, take the time to review it closely and carefully compare it to your other credit information such as past bills and mortgage information. If there are discrepancies, start a vigorous letter campaign immediately   to make the company change the information.   This will, of course, be much easier if you have several correct reports to help prove your point that your information has turned sour. A lot of patience and determination will be required if you do have to "go into combat" with the credit reporting bureaus.   The problem will be compounded because the companies share information with one another and an error in one could result in several databases becoming corrupted.

Above all, good luck.

Action Steps

Since most of this chapter consists of specific, detailed actions you should take to protect your vital data from the Y2K Crisis, this section will be relatively short, There are some things worth mentioning, however, just to summarize.

Spike Date Precautions

If you will take a moment to review the Spike Date Precautions from previous chapters you will see many of them can be summarized into the following prescription:

1. *Protect your existing data by obtaining and main-
    taining a hard copy version in your Vital Informa-
    tion Portfolio.*

2. *Avoid the creation of new data during those periods
    when it has the greatest risk of becoming contami-
    nated or lost (i.e.,on Spike Dates).*

If you follow this advice, you will take every possible
action to avoid giving any new vital data to any of the following:

the federal government
state and local government agencies.
your employer
your debtors
your medical service providers
the legal system
the banking system
your investment structure
the educational system
credit reporting companies

... and so on

Continuation Precautions

In addition to the information contained in the main
body of this chapter, there are a few additional items
worth mentioning.

Don't accept anything which expires in the years "99"
or "00." This includes documents such as driver's licenses, parking passes, credit cards, building access cards, library cards, subscriptions, memberships in organizations
and so forth. Accepting these documents means you are

allowing the creation of personal data which will be entered into databases likely to be Y2K impaired.

Let others know about Y2K. The more people who voice concern about Y2K, the better chance we have of overcoming and surviving the problem. This point is so important, all of Chapter 11 is devoted to the issue. Talk about the Year 2000 Problem whenever you have the chance. Write letters to decision makers. Get involved in your community. Talk to your employer.

Be especially alert about protecting the vital data of children born in 1998, 1999 and 2000. Their data will be at special risk. In fact, avoid having children during these years if possible. (I'll bet you didn't expect to find birth control advice in this book, huh?)

"It's been a hard day's night,
and I been working like a dog."

"It's Been a Hard Day's Night" - the Beatles

Chapter 8

Y2K And
Employment

Imagine

One of the greatest personal threats of the Y2K Crisis is
the impact it could have on your job. It could affect your
pay, the benefits your receive (including your medical insurance) or your pension. It could even threaten the very
existence of your employer. Here is what things might be
like.

*It's Friday and today is payday. Just home from
work, you're standing at the kitchen counter picking through the day's mail. As expected, there's
your paycheck, right on time as usual, "Those folks
in accounting have really got their act together,"
you say to yourself. Setting the envelope aside, you
scan the rest of the mail. After tossing the junk
mail and reading a letter from your mom, you go
back and open up the pay envelope. It doesn't register right away and you have to read the pay stub
twice before it starts to come clear. Your pay is less*

than half as much as usual and everything else is screwed up as well. No leave is shown and you know you've got over forty days on the books. And there's no sick leave shown either. There's no clue why everything is such a mess and you wonder if you should cancel out on tonight's dinner and a movie.

As you ponder this mystery, the telephone rings. It's your sister and she's crying. Through the sobs, she manages to tell you that she got laid off because her company lost a big government contract. This is a real shocker because the contract had three years left to run. She explains that the government program her company was supporting was canceled because the funding was pulled. The rumor is that her company might even go out of business.

Still dazed by this double dose of bad news, you pick up today's newspaper and head for the couch. The front page story is about a local manufacturing company with 3000 employees which is being sued by its stockholders.

This chapter will concentrate on how Y2K could affect what goes on within your employer's company and its computers. We will also look at a few external factors that could affect your employment. We look first at the heart of the matter. Your paycheck.

Pay Up

Getting your paycheck into your pocket is a pretty complex process. So much so, in fact, that most employers use computers to handle the process. This is true whether the payroll process is handled in house or is farmed out to an accounting firm or a payroll service. Governments are the main culprit in causing this complexity. They require deductions to be made from each paycheck for the following:

- *Federal income tax withholding*

- *State income tax withholding (if applicable)*

- *Social Security payments*

- *Unemployment insurance payments*

- *Workman's Compensation insurance*

- *Medicare payments*

But that's not the whole story by any means. There are probably several other accounting entries on your pay stub some of which are indirectly the result of government influence. They are loosely called "fringe benefits," and might include some of the following:

- *paid vacation*   - *paid sick leave*
- *pension plan*   - *401 (k) plan*
- *profit sharing plan*   - *stock purchase plan*
- *payroll savings plan*   - *health insurance*
- *life insurance*   - *disability insurance*

Many of these are regulated by the government or are allowed to be provided to you tax free. There has been a strong trend in the past twenty years, for example, for employers to load their payroll up with these tax free benefits instead of increasing the pay of their employees.

This trend is beneficial to both employer and employee but it does have one subtle and important side effect. It has added tremendously to the complexity of the payroll process and has contributed significantly to the automation of that process. Since all payroll information is date related, payroll software is highly susceptible to Y2K problems.

Pay Off

Malfunctions in your employer's payroll software could affect you in many ways. You could receive the wrong amount in your paycheck or your deductions could be wrong. A problem in your pay would almost certainly be detected by you immediately if you are careful in inspecting your check or the direct deposit receipt you get in the mail. All you have to do is be aware. Incorrect deductions could be more difficult to detect, however, and the secondary problems arising from them could go undetected for a long time or even forever. For example, if an incorrect amount is deducted for your 401 (k) plan you might never know the difference. Serious underpayments to the Internal Revenue Service could be very unpleasant for you as well. If your income taxes are underpaid by too much, not only could you owe significant taxes but penalties could start to kick in as well. This kind of problem could be extremely difficult to detect.

Record Breaking

Employee personnel records are another potential source of Y2K grief. With the probable exception of the smaller companies, many employers maintain these records in computerized databases. Although Y2K errors in these are probably unlikely to cost you your job, you could be denied a promotion, a choice assignment or a pay raise. Examples of specific areas of your employment information which could become corrupted are:

- *hiring date*
- *leave records*
- *training records*
- *transfer records*
- *401(k) fund selections*
- *time sheet records*

- *promotion dates*
- *sick leave records*
- *pay schedule*
- *health insurance records*
- *task assignments*
- *vesting status for pensions, or stock options*

just to name a few.

Threats to Business

The greatest threat to your employment, of course, is the outright loss of your job. Experts predict that many companies will go out of business because of the Y2K Crisis. First let's look at how many companies that might be.

The most thorough study of the expected economic effect of Y2K has been done by Capers Jones, chairman and founder of Software Productivity Research, in Burlington, Massachusetts. Mr. Jones is a software legend who has written many books and articles on the software industry and profession. He is also a frequent speaker at large software conferences and seminars. In a study published by his company and entitled, <u>The Economic Impact of the Year 2000 Computer Software Problem</u>, he estimates:

- *1% of very large companies will fail. By this estimate, five of the Fortune 500 companies will go under.*

- *5-7% of midsize companies will fail. These are defined as companies which employ from one thousand to ten thousand employees. There are about thirty thousand such companies in the United States.*

- *3% of very small companies will fail. Very small is defined as having fewer than a hundred employees. There are around six million such companies.*

I won't subject you to all the number-crunching but my quick research leads me to believe this would result in unemployment of around ten or eleven million people. This is in addition to the "regular" unemployment figures.

The bottom line here, of course, is that your company and, therefore, your job are in significant jeopardy.

Why, Oh Why?

Exactly what will cause these business failures? As I see it, there will be four major causes. The first is the disruption of ordinary business activities which are completely dependent on the use of computers and which must be done virtually on a daily basis in order for any business to survive. Here are some examples of these kinds of activities:

- *accounts receivable - if you can't invoice or bill your customers, they can't pay you.*

- *accounts payable - paying your bills to the electric company, the landlord or the tax man is obviously critical to business survival.*

- *payroll - few businesses could survive a single pay cycle without paying employees.*

- *purchasing - retailers are particularly susceptible here. This function is often totally automated in many modern companies such as Wal-Mart, Sears etc.*

- *shipping - if you can't get your product out the door you can't get paid either.*

There are many other ordinary business activities which will be disrupted by the Y2K Problem and some will threaten the existence of particular companies. The above are considered the most representative however.

Dependencies

The second major cause of business failures will be from sources external to the company. Many companies will go under not because they themselves suffer from Year 2000 problems but because enterprises upon which they are dependent have Y2K problems. For example, a company could have all their Y2K ducks in a perfect row and still go out of business because one or more of the following have Y2K problems of their own:

The bank - certainly it would cause a major problem if a company's bank went under but there is another, hidden danger. Many businesses are heavily dependent on a running line of credit (LOC) with the bank to provide funds for day to day operations. If this line tightens up or disappears it will be disastrous for many firms. I predict that many banks will just plain get scared when the Y2K problems start and LOC's will become both expensive and scarce. Many businesses will be jeopardized by this threat alone.

   Vendors and suppliers - manufacturers seldom make all the parts for the things they sell. If one of their key suppliers goes out of business with a Y2K problem, it could cause severe consequences. An automobile manufacturer, for example, could easily be dependent on 500 or more vendors to provide everything from tires to light bulbs. One of the big car companies recently shut down for several weeks because a brake manufacturer went on strike.

   Customers - If your customers go away, you fail. If you only have a few customers or even one, you are in even greater danger. I know many small defense contractors, for example, who are completely dependent on a single contract with one government agency for the existence of the entire company. If your employer has only a few customers, be very wary.

   Distribution network - companies which are heavily dependent on transportation services are in harm's way as well. If your business depends on a constant flow of materials shipped in or out of the firm by air, truck or rail service, it is susceptible to disruptions of that flow if those transportation companies experience Y2K problems. Transportation relies very heavily on computers for the scheduling, tracking and maintenance of their carriers and Y2K will strike all of these functions.

   Communications providers - many companies simply can't do business without telephones. Services such as the Internet, fax, radio, television, cellular phones and pagers are included here as well.

   Data providers - some companies are dependent on others for a constant flow of information used in the business. Real estate agents and brokers, for example, need access to the data contained in the Multiple Listing Service (MLS) which is a database of all properties for sale or rent in their area.   Companies which do lots of direct mail business are highly dependent on computerized mailing lists of clients and their addresses.

Legal

Thirdly, the legal costs of Y2K are expected to exceed the cost of fixing the problem itself. The lawsuits will fly like snowflakes. Everybody in sight will be sued. Computer and software vendors, company officers and directors, companies which sell tools and services used to repair Y2K problems, the government, companies that use computers, auditing firms, and the beat goes on. Class action lawsuits will fly against the big companies with the deep pockets. You will see an instant replay of the breast implant story of a few years back and the tobacco damages lawsuits of today.

Big Bucks

Finally, fixing the Y2K Problem is going to be very expensive: over $2,000 for every man, woman and child in the country according to Capers Jones in the report mentioned above Prudential Life Insurance plans to spend around a hundred twenty million dollars on the problem for example. That's about 600 people working on the problem full time for two years. Many companies won't be able to afford the price tag and will simply close their doors.

Risky Business

Some kinds of business have a greater year 2000 risk than others. This next section will identify some business types that fit into this category. If you are employed by an organization which fits any of the descriptions below, you should seriously consider changing jobs. If your employer fits two or more of these categories - RUN. Here's a laundry list of these kinds of enterprises:

Midrange companies - for reasons outlined above.

Non-profit enterprises - charities, churches, trade associations, etc. These organizations are often woefully understaffed, underqualified and underfunded for any kind of computer crisis.

State and local governments are at special risk. The resources they can bring to bear will be inadequate to the task in many cases.

Businesses located in major metropolitan areas have a special risk factor due to the threat of civil disturbances and the widespread disruption of critical infrastructure factors.

Heavily computerized enterprises are at special risk. If your place of employment consists mostly of people sitting at computer terminals, whatever their purpose or the nature of the work, you have a higher risk.

Businesses with an overseas orientation. If your company is intensely dependent on overseas suppliers or customers, you have greater risk because those areas are further behind the curve in addressing the Y2K problem than we are in the United States.

Y2K Boom - or Bust?

Will Y2K cause a recession or, worse yet, the next Great Depression? Many Y2K thinkers believe so but I hold something of a contrarian view. I do think there will be major employment disruptions and many business failures but there is a silver lining all around those gloomy clouds.

For one thing, there is going to be a downright gold rush for computer programmers. If you have any talent in this area, get ready for the good times by learning an OLD computer language such as COBOL.

I believe there will also be an employment explosion for people who can manually do all that previously auto-mated work. My favorite guesses would be bookkeeping, accounting, filing, scheduling etc. If you can do any of these things by hand you will be in great demand. Schools that teach these kinds of manual skills will also do very well. Temporary agencies are another good bet because many companies will have computer problems for a few months and then get back on line gradually. Se-curity companies will also be in big demand because there will be widespread failures of electronic alarm systems.

Overall, the Y2K Crisis is likely to result in something of a resurrection of manual labor. It will be the only way many businesses will be able to survive. Even though things will be tough and many businesses will disappear, there will also be plenty of work available for those will-ing to go back to the old way for a while until the prob-lems get cleaned up.

Action Steps

Spike Date Precautions

It is critical for you to find out the end of your employer's fiscal year. The fiscal year end that occurs in 1998 and the one that occurs in 1999 will be two of your most important Personal Spike Dates. You should avoid all significant employment related transactions around those two dates. This includes such things as starting a new job, leaving a job, taking a transfer, getting a pay raise or a promotion, taking a qualification exam, undergoing important training or retiring.

I also recommend you stay home from work on all Spike Dates and I further suggest you take leave for a week on either side of your two Personal Spike Dates.

Parking and access passes will go haywire on and around Spike Dates (which is another good reason to stay home). Replace passes that expire in "99" or "00" if possible.

Continuation Precautions

If you are employed by one of the high risk employers described above, start taking action now to get yourself moved into one of the less risky types of businesses.

Closely inspect all employment documents for correct date information. Don't accept anything dated in the years "99" or "00". This would include parking and building access passes, employee identification passes, and automobile parking decals, etc.

Go to night school and learn a manual skill. These will sell at a premium when things get tough. This would include such skills as auto mechanics, sewing, home making skills, bookkeeping, accounting, carpentry, electrical work, plumbing, appliance repair and gardening to name a few.

Inspect carefully and keep a copy of all pay stubs and all pension and 401(k) statements. The key thing to be alert for is unexplained changes. If the amount deducted for income tax changes, for example, but the amount of your pay is the same, ask the payroll folks why the change was made.

Talk to your employer about the Year 2000 Problem to determine if he is getting prepared. Buy him a copy of this book. Better yet, buy a copy of this book for everybody you know. (There's an order form in the back.)

Get a complete copy of your pay and personnel record. Update the copy every six months and add this information to your Vital Information Portfolio.

If you have influence with your employer or if he or she is "Y2K enlightened," bring up the subject of business interruption insurance to cover losses during Spike Date disruptions. If you get it now, and get it long term, it may be less expensive than waiting until the problem is better known and understood. Also try to get this type of employer to consider holding "Y2K fire drills". It is good, sound emergency planning to practice what you would do when your computers go crazy.

Chapter 9

Y2K And Your Personal Well-being

Imagine

You're worried.

It's late Saturday morning and you're returning to your home in a quiet suburb fifteen miles outside the city. You've just come from the shopping center and it was <u>not</u> a pleasant trip. You had intended to do your grocery shopping for the week but you've come home mostly empty-handed. It was an astonishing sight at the store - they were running out of food right in front of your eyes. The milk, eggs, bread and meat were already gone and the canned food was going as fast as people could get it into their carts.

The most scary part, though, was the people. Anger, fear and near panic were obvious everywhere. One guy in the checkout line had his cart stacked high with meat. The other people were cursing him and demanding to know why he was taking so much when they didn't have any. It was about to get really nasty when two policeman showed up. They took most of the man's meat and divided it up amongst the other people waiting in line. As you left the store, a fistfight was about to break out at another checkout stand.

Hurrying through the parking lot, you noticed several people who had just come from inside who were selling the groceries they had just bought for twice what they paid. They had both bread and milk so you bought some. It made you mad having to pay so much but you were glad to get the food, even at that price.

Needing gas, you drove around the corner to the gas station and got your second big shock of the day. The line was a block long! When you finally made it to the head of the line after a half hour wait, there was a sign posted on the pump. "Ten Gallon Limit," it proclaimed. "No exceptions."

The Year 2000 Crisis will pose a real physical threat to many people. For some, this danger will come from disruptions in the marketplace which will halt the flow of basic economic goods such as food, fuel and energy. For others, the danger will come from interruptions in essential government services such as police and fire protection. For others it will come from the most terrifying effect of all - civil disorders, rioting and, potentially, open warfare in the streets. This chapter examines those dangers and recommends steps you can take to protect yourself from them.

Necessity is the Mother

The necessities of life such as food, clothing, shelter and transportation come to us through the most efficient economic machine the world has ever known. Indeed, it works so well, it is virtually transparent to us. Were it not for the big trucks on the highway we would forget it entirely. Just like we seldom think about the pipes under the ground that bring water into our homes. Until they burst, that is.

The fundamental technology that makes this marvelous efficiency possible is - computers. The massive farm machines that plant, tend and harvest the food are controlled by computers. The plants that process the raw foodstuff and turn it into Twinkies and beefsteaks are managed and operated by computers. As are the trucks and ships and planes that deliver it to the stores. It is the computer that manages the everyday activities of those stores from pricing the eggs, to putting the beans on the shelves to totaling up the customer's bill at the checkout stand and then ordering new stock from the wholesaler. And then, of course, the banking system gets involved all along the way as all these players in the food chain transfer funds amongst themselves to make payment for everything. This reliance on computers goes right down to the final customer who pays for those bananas or that shirt with a debit card which talks to a computer to clear the transaction.

It Only Takes One

All of these computers are vulnerable to the Year 2000 Problem, of course, which means that every single link in the chain of distribution is weak. When you think of it, this is an amazing concept. The idea of a strong chain with one weak link is a common metaphor. It stands for a thing believed to be strong and invincible but which has a single, unknown, tragically fatal flaw which manifests itself at the worst possible time, leading to disaster. Y2K produces the amazing situation of discovering that the entire chain is made not of carbon steel but paper mache' instead and that every single link is not only capable of, but highly prone to failure.

I personally find this to be one of the most frightening aspects of Y2K. Our system of distributing goods is so marvelous that we become convinced it could never fail. Y2K, however, reveals it to be so fragile that it is hard to imagine it continuing to operate without major disruptions. These disruptions in the flow of the basic necessities will cause three very predictable results right out of a basic economics textbook.

One For You and One For Me

The first of these predictable actions is the imposition of rationing and price controls. Reacting to a crescendo in the press about "price gouging," and "greedy businessmen," and demands to "do something," the government will lurch into action. Claiming to know what is "fair" in the marketplace, they will dictate who gets the goods and how much will be paid. Throughout history, government has always attempted these measures. They always fail, however, because not even massive force can repeal the law of supply and demand. Even knowing they will fail, however, they will take these steps. The bottom line is that even though rationing and price controls are unworkable economic policy, they are the only course of action possible in a political sense. Accordingly, you can be dead certain they will happen.

Hey, Buddy

The predictable (and natural) reaction to rationing and price controls will be the rise of black markets. These illegal marketplaces are common whenever there is a limited supply of something that is intensely desired by many people. Ticket scalpers at sporting events are a relatively harmless example. On the darker side are the bathtub gin and bootleg whiskey of seventy years ago and the world-wide, multi-billion dollar market in illegal drugs of today. The point is that black markets will exist wherever there is sufficient demand for a product whether government approves them or not.

This economic phenomenon will apply to bread, milk, eggs and hamburger just as much as it applies to World Series tickets or bags of marijuana. When food or gasoline become scarce and the government steps in to regulate their availability and price, entrepreneurs will leap into the fray with amazing speed. This is not a treatise on the morality of black markets. I just want you to understand that they will likely proliferate during the Y2K Crisis.

What's Mine is Mine

The other predictable result of shortages in essential economic goods will be hoarding. When desirable goods become hard to get, people naturally try to obtain more than they need immediately and keep it for a rainy day. Or even to possibly build up stock for making an entry into a black market. Indeed, hoarding and black marketing are somewhat related in this sense and it is certainly possible that the government will attempt to control this activity as well. (With little success, if history is any lesson). I am going to be judgmental about hoarding, however. I am completely in favor of it and, indeed, it is one of my strongest recommendations for you to take in preparation for the Y2K Challenge.

Critical Action Step #4 -
Store Necessities

The moral justification for you to keep a storage of essential goods is that it is good for the community and it is good for you and your family. Here's how:

When the supermarket and the gas station start running short, you will not be standing in line competing for those scarce goods. In other words, by building up a storage of scarce foods now, you will be part of the solution instead of contributing to the problem.

Your storage program will save money in three ways. First, buying necessities in quantity for storage purposes is more economical because you will be buying in bulk. Secondly, when these essential items become scarce, they will increase dramatically in price. Buying today will be less expensive. Finally, even though inflation has been pretty low over the last ten years or so (2-3%), it has not disappeared. Even at these low rates, prices would rise nearly 10% over a three year period. Buying now reduces your cost in the long run.

Your stored goods are a terrific investment. They can never go down in value because that can of beans is always going to be worth a can of beans regardless of its price in the marketplace. These items can, however, increase in value immensely if things get really tough on the outside. Finally, there is the insurance value.

Y2K Insurance

A solid storage program is the greatest insurance policy money can buy. It will give you protection in exactly the most critical, fundamentally important areas of your life, e.g. food, water, clothing, and energy. If these commodities become scarce due to marketplace disruptions, you will be immune. If your job disappears or is interrupted, you will still be able to provide these necessities for your family. If you can't physically get to work or to the grocery store because of transportation problems or access problems in your office building or factory, you will still have the things you need the most. When the ATM's and credit cards and banks stop working you'll still be able to eat. When the power or the water go off for a week or two, again, you will be part of the solution instead of being part of the problem.

Getting Personal

Let me briefly relate my personal experience with storing food and other commodities. At several points during my military service, I was often separated from my home and family for extended periods. With a large family, I was always concerned that something might go wrong while I was away. Then I read a bestselling book by Howard Ruff entitled, How to Prosper During the Coming Bad Years. This exceptional book inspired me to make a number of changes in my life including setting up a food storage program (in fact, many of the recommendations included in this chapter are based directly on this great book). My wife and I researched the subject and then gradually put together a year's supply of food and other basic necessities as I will describe momentarily.

The result for me was a tremendous peace of mind. Even when I was at sea halfway around the world I knew that no matter what, my family was protected against most kinds of disasters. Which is exactly what an insurance policy is supposed to do. I guess the strongest testimony I can give about a storage program is this. Even if there was no Y2K crisis coming, I would still recommend that you store food and other necessities.

How Much?

A good storage program should be able to provide all the members of your family with six months worth of necessities. What's magic about six months? Not a thing. But if the primary breadwinner in your family becomes unemployed due to the Y2K Crisis, six months would likely give sufficient basic protection while other income arrangements are made. Remember, the purpose of insurance is to protect against the bad things that could happen. Indeed, if you can afford the expense and if you have the room, a <u>twelve month</u> storage program is not a bad idea.

Shelf Life

Your personal storehouse should consist of all the things that are critical to your well-being and even some things that would just simply add to your comfort. Here are some of the things you should consider:

<u>Food</u>. Store bulk staples such as grain, rice and beans. If packed properly, they can be kept virtually indefinitely. Canned foods of all types and freeze-dried (or dehydrated) meals such as those used by campers and hunters are excellent but should be rotated through usage because they will not keep well for very long periods. You should also include a range of vitamin supplements and don't forget to include pet food.

<u>Water</u>. Store bottled water for drinking and cooking and plain old tap water for washing. This will probably be the most bulky part of your program. A tip - a waterbed is a great place to store water for washing purposes.

Commodities. The best way to figure out what should be on this list of everyday items is to save and analyze a couple of months worth of store receipts. This part of your storage should include such things as toilet articles, clothing, critical auto parts such as spark plugs and a couple of spare tires etc. Also included here should be a supply of off-the-shelf medications and any prescription medicines you might need. Work with your doctor to set up a way for you to rotate prescription medications. Oh yeah, be sure to remember toilet paper.

Emergency Supplies. This would include items such as batteries, candles, matches. a lantern, flashlights, a small radio, a basic tool box and a first aid kit. A good, general purpose survival book would be a good addition to add to your library. A Boy Scout Manual would work fine.

Cash. I also recommend that your storage program include cash sufficient to pay three months bills. Do not keep this money in a safe deposit box. Its purpose is to protect you against economic disturbances that might interrupt your normal cash flow. Some of these disturbances could include difficulties with the banking system so this emergency cash should be kept on hand where you have control of it. Private safe deposit facilities would be a safe alternative if available.

I have not gone into any great detail here on how to set up and maintain your storage program because this is not a book on that subject. I just wanted to include enough information to get you started. There are plenty of good books on methodology and I strongly suggest you do some research on the subject and then get started. One of the best ways to start getting smart on this matter is to get a book titled <u>Making the Best of Basics: Family Preparedness Handbook</u> by James Talmage Stevens. Information about this excellent book is provided in Chapter 12. Appendix D in this Survival Guide provides a directory of emergency preparedness vendors.

Critical Action Step # 5 - Buy Gold and Silver Coins

The next major precaution you should take to protect yourself and your family is to own some good old fashioned money - in the form of gold and silver coins. Before I go any further, let me say clearly that I am not a gold nut and I am not predicting the end of our world as we know it. As I indicated in Chapter 5 on the Financial Implications of Y2K, I do believe there will be serious disruptions in the economy and in the stock market. These spasms may be short lived or they may be real stem-winders. No one has any way of knowing at this point.

The point of this recommendation is precisely the same point I made about food storage. Get some insurance against what might happen. These gold and silver coins are <u>not an investment</u>; they are insurance against disaster. The best thing that could possibly happen is that you will never need these coins. You should not care one whit whether the price of gold or silver goes up or down while you own them. The purpose of the coins is to give you stable purchasing power that will not be corrupted or influenced by the Y2K Crisis. If banks close or even go under and you cannot get to your money through the financial infrastructure (ATM's, credit cards, checks etc.), gold and silver coins will provide you a way to conduct your critical economic affairs. Such as purchasing gas or food.

All that Glitters

It is surprisingly easy to purchase gold and silver coins. In most places, all you need to do is look in the phone book under, believe it or not, "Coin Dealers." There are only a couple of things you need to be aware of. First, buy coins for their precious metal content only and not for their numismatic value. These coins are not collector's items. They have value only because they contain gold or silver. This means you do not want any coins that are individually wrapped. The second important thing is that you do not want privately issued, limited edition coins or bars such as those sold by the Franklin Mint and similar companies. What you want are common date coins issued by a government as currency.

Up until 1964, dimes, quarters, half dollars and one dollar coins contained 90% pure silver by weight. One dollar's worth of coins from those years, in any combination of denominations, contains about .72 ounces of silver. Dimes, quarters and dollar coins minted after 1964 contain no silver at all. Half dollars minted from 1965 to 1970 contain 40% silver. The pre-65 coins are the ones I recommend. These coins are called "Junk Silver," because they have no value as collectible coins. They are simply a form of silver. I recommend these coins because of their convenience and their safety. Since they are minted by the government they are easily recognizable, very difficult to forge and the amount of silver they contain is known with certainty.

Everything Else That Glitters

Gold coins provide the other half of your "survival stash." Again, you should not purchase coins with numismatic value. All you are interested in is the gold cont-

ent. These kinds of coins are often called "bullion coins."
Any of the following types is fine; American Eagle, Aus-
trian Corona, South African Kruggerand, Canadian Maple
Leaf or Mexican Peso. These can usually be purchased in
various weights such as 1/20, 1/10, 1/4, 1/2 or one ounce.
Gold bullion coins have one significant advantage over
silver junk coins. You can pack much more value into
the same space since one ounce of gold sells for about 75
times as much as an ounce of silver.

Details

My recommendation is that you hold about $5,000
(purchase value, not face value) in coins, split equally between gold and silver, for each member of your family.
Take full possession of your coins and do not buy them on
margin. Remember, these coins are not an investment.
They are long term "survival insurance." Also, for privacy sake, I strongly recommend that you do not use any
checks in purchasing the coins. This probably means you
will have to buy them in several steps because there is a
federal form that must be submitted for cash transactions
greater than $10,000. For this reason, limit any single pur-
chase to less than this amount. As mentioned earlier, do
not store these coins in a bank safe deposit box. Either
keep them at home or in a private safe deposit facility.

The next topic is the most unpleasant of this book and
in all likelihood the most controversial as well - the physical danger of the Year 2000 Crisis.

Eight Cans of Worms

There is a great danger of increased crime associated
with the Year 2000 Problem. Many scenarios could produce this result but one in particular seems the most like-

ly to me. That is the high probability there will be serious disruptions in the disbursement of federal entitlement benefits within the inner cities. This includes benefits such as food stamps, Aid to Families with Dependent Children (AFDC), and subsidized housing. Recent legislation to massively reform the nation's welfare system will contribute significantly to the problem. Eight factors will work together to create the problem. They are these:

1. *Most federal welfare benefits are implemented, managed and disbursed by the state governments.*

2. *Each state's welfare system is different.*

3. *In July 1998, many states will begin to encounter the first serious Y2K difficulties due to the database "99" problem. (Review Chapters 2 and 5 and Appendix A for more details on this important Y2K effect.) As a result the states have <u>less time</u> to prepare for Y2K than most other enterprises.*

4. *The state governments lag behind the federal government in both awareness of and preparation for the Y2K Crisis.*

5. *The states will have difficulty raising funds for Y2K software repair expenses because most have strict balanced budget laws. Accordingly, Y2K funding must be taken out of other planned expenditures. This will be very unpopular politically because the beneficiaries of these programs will have to lose benefits to raise money for Y2K.*

6. *The states' computer systems are networked together with the federal computer systems. This*

means there are 52 Y2K related welfare problems to deal with instead of one.   (Federal government plus fifty states and the District of Columbia.)

7.   *The methods used to repair the states' welfare computers are highly dependent on how the federal government fixes its computer software. Some of the work cannot even start until the federal government decides what they are going to do and provides guidance to the states.*

8.   *The new welfare reform legislation requires significant changes in how entitlement programs are operated.   These changes will necessitate massive alterations in both the federal government's computer software and in that used by all fifty states.and in the District of Columbia.Many technically overwhelming decisions must be made in implementing these massive software changes.*

The states face immense challenges in preparing for the Y2K Crisis. Millions of lines of computer code contain fatal errors and must be repaired and tested prior to the summer of 1998. The work must start immediately and everything must be done exactly right in order to avert a catastrophe. Attempting to implement welfare reform at the same time will prove disastrous. From a technical standpoint, I believe it is impossible to do both. Unfortunately, politics rather than good sense will drive this issue and the attempt will be made. In my judgment, that decision will prove to be disastrous.

Stick 'Em Up

The results could be chaotic. If the disruption of benefits to the inner cities is serious there could be widespread rioting, looting, arson and property crime. The conflagration would almost certainly spread to the nearby suburbs as the mobs run out of food and other necessities. The streets of the large metropolitan areas would be turned into virtual war zones. Martial law is probable. The economic impact would be severe as the cities burn down. Panic will ensue and refugees will leave the cities by the hundreds of thousands. Businesses and residences in the cities and the near suburbs will be devastated.

Carl Rowan, a prominent, liberal, African-American journalist, recently published a book entitled, <u>The Coming Race War in America: A Wakeup Call</u>. Although reading this book will not be a pleasant experience, I strongly suggest you add it to your Y2K library. Now, I freely admit my political views are far to the right of Mr. Rowan's, but I do believe he is an honest and sincere man. You need to read this book because it is a blueprint for what could happen in the cities at the peak of the Y2K Catastrophe. Expect to have your pants scared right off. Rowan's stunning premise is that racial hatred has us teetering on the brink of open warfare in the United States. It is entirely possible that Y2K combined with a botched welfare reform effort could provide the match for Rowan's can of gasoline.

Critical Action Step # 6 -
Move Away From the Cities

This is the toughest of the six Critical Action Steps if you live in or near a big city. Following it will be very difficult for many readers of this Survival Guide. I would not offer it at all except that I am scared to death of what Y2K could bring. I will probably be branded as a nut and an alarmist by many readers and reviewers of this book entirely because of this paragraph That doesn't matter, however. I accept the criticism because I must tell you what I honestly think will happen and what I really think you should do to prepare for Y2K. To do otherwise would be to betray my heart and your confidence.

Mind you, I am not suggesting that you lock up the house or the apartment or the business and get out of town for a few days while the storm blows over. Your actions must be much stronger than that. Sell all property within thirty miles of a major city. Pack up your belongings and your family and get away while it is possible to do so. Do this now before property values drop like a rock. Start life anew in a small community where welfare programs are a relative rarity.   Live in a community where the local churches and charities will be able to take care of the needy if things get really bad because of Y2K.

If you work in the city or nearby suburbs, try to get transferred or change jobs. Your employment situation will also become endangered by the civil discord resulting from Y2K.

Up In Arms

Should you get a gun? Arm yourself and your family? In a word - no. I'm trying to show you how to avoid the warfare, not become a part of it. The principal strategy should be to get off the battlefield. Don't misunderstand, I'm not anti-gun. I own guns and am strongly opposed to gun control. We had guns of all types in my home when I was a child and hunting and shooting were part of my life. I also don't have any problem at all with people protecting themselves using firearms. I would do the same if I had to. Nonetheless, I don't recommend that guns become an important part of your strategy for getting through the Y2K Crisis. The best thing you can do to assure the safety of you and your family is to put yourselves in a safe place.

Dictator Bill

What will the government do if things really do blow up in the cities? The first step after the local police fail to control the situation will be a frantic call to the National Guard. This action can be taken by the Governor of the state you live in. If the National Guard is insufficient to handle matters, there is another, much more serious step past this one. The President can declare a national emergency and thereby invoke a set of amazingly draconian measures which would, in essence, make him the dictator of the United States.

These measures include the "Defense Production Act of 1950" and Executive Orders (EO) 12656, "Assignment of Emergency Preparedness Responsibilities," 12472, "Assignment of National Security and Emergency Preparedness Telecommunications Functions," and 12919 "National Defense Industrial Resources Preparedness."

These largely unknown and little understood laws, approved by Congress and signed into law by a succession of Presidents from Truman to Clinton, give the Executive Branch of government a long list of really eye-popping powers to take over just about all aspects of American life.

Here are some of the actions that could be taken. Each instance is followed the actual language from the law.

Take control of all radio and television stations and all telephone companies. Confiscate personal communications equipment including cellular phones; CB, ham and short-wave radios and Internet servers.

"(Develop plans for) the mobilization and use of the Nation's commercial, government, and <u>privately owned telecommunications resources,</u> (my emphasis) in order to meet national security or emergency preparedness requirements." (EO 12472)

Take over all forms of transportation train, bus, air, subway, trucking, shipping and railroad companies and appropriate personal vehicles.

"(Provide for the) emergency management and control of civil transportation resources and systems, <u>including privately owned automobiles,</u> (my emphasis) urban mass transit (and) inter modal transportation systems." (EO 12656)

Take control of water production and treatment facilities and ration all water from whatever source.

"(Develop) plans for the management, control, and allocation of all usable waters from all sources within the jurisdiction of the United States." (EO 12656)

Conscript civilians into military service or to work in essential (as determined by the government) factories, plants or laboratories, farms, etc. This could include computer programmers for use in working on Year 2000 computer problems.

"Develop ... plans and systems to ensure that the Nation's human resources are available to meet essential military <u>and civilian needs</u> (my emphasis) in national security emergencies." (EO 12656)

And in a separate paragraph,

"Develop plans and issue guidance to ensure effective use of civilian work force resources during national security emergencies." (EO 12656)

Appropriate all power plants and decide unilaterally which communities and which industries will be allowed the use of electrical power.

"(D)evelop ... plans (for the) allocation of all energy resource requirements for national defense and essential civilian needs to assure national security emergency preparedness." (EO 12656)

Take control of all medical facilities and ration all medical services.

"Develop national plans to set priorities and allocate health, mental health, and medical services' resources among civilian and military claimants." (EO 12656)

Impose wage and price controls on all workers and businesses.

"(D)evelop plans and procedures for wage, salary, and benefit costs stabilization during national security emergencies." (EO 12656)

Take control of all private means of transportation as well as private warehouse facilities.

"(Develop plans for the) operation of privately owned (my emphasis) railroads, motor carriers, inland

waterway transportation systems, and public storage facilities and services in national security emergencies." (EO 12656)

Take over all stock and commodity exchanges and markets such as the New York Stock Exchange and the NASDAQ. Control the value of all stocks, bonds, mutual funds and other investment vehicles.

"(Develop) emergency financial control plans and regulations for trading of stocks and commodities." (EO 12656)

How Could this Happen?

The President does not need the approval of Congress to invoke a national emergency. He only needs to declare it to be so. Could Congress take any action to stop him? Well, the law gives them the power to <u>review</u> the actions after six months. So, what it amounts to is we just have to trust the president's judgment and character. If that makes you feel comfortable, I have a real nice bridge in Brooklyn I would like to talk to you about.

What might constitute a "national emergency?" Here is what the law says,

"A national security emergency is any occurrence, including natural disaster, military attack, <u>technological emergency</u>, (my emphasis) or other emergency, that seriously degrades or seriously threatens the national security of the United States." (EO 12656)

In other words, it can be anything the president wants it to be and the Year 2000 Computer Problem would certainly qualify under the "technological emergency" clause.

Action Steps

Spike Date Precautions

Since a great deal of this chapter presents recommendations on how to protect yourself during the worst of the Y2K Crisis, this section will be fairly brief. The first and most important is to <u>stay home</u> on Spike Dates. (See Critical Action Step #2.) If there are problems with the delivery of essential services such as electricity or water to your home it is best if you are there to manage the situation. This is particularly true during "environmentally challenging" periods such as the hottest time of summer or the coldest time of winter. These are the times when your home is the most "stressed" by the weather and most vulnerable to damage from the loss of services.

The threat of civil disorder is also higher around Spike Dates. It is best to draw yourself and your family back into the cocoon a little just as a precaution. Stay at home and don't subject yourself to driving through urban areas for example. For the same reasons, it is also a time during which you wouldn't want your children in school.

Continuation Precautions

Physical security is a paramount concern if civil strife breaks out. There are a number of things you might consider. Protect your home with a security system and buy a dog. A large dog. Personal protection devices such as pepper spray are also suggested. Consider living in a guarded community. Don't depend too heavily on local police and firemen because they may not be there due to pay, pension or personnel problems.

Develop a privacy habit. Keep your entire storage program to yourself because those who don't prepare are going to want what you have. Be extremely private about storing food, emergency cash, gold and silver for obvious reasons. You should also protect your privacy when purchasing these commodities. Pay in cash and use amounts less than ten thousand dollars so the transaction will not be reportable to the government. There is simply no need for anyone outside your family to have knowledge of your affairs. Also be very careful about what information you divulge to children about these matter. Take into account that they do not have the constraint and judgment adults might have and will not understand the importance of maintaining privacy.

Monitor the entertainment industry closely. It could provide you with a key indicator of how bad any Y2K panic might be. As soon as you see any prime time, television movies or specials about the Y2K crisis, your antennae should begin to quiver. Pay very close attention to that signal. A feature film or a best selling book would have the same effect but would probably manifest itself in a slower fashion.

"I read the news today, oh boy."

"A Day in the Life" - the Beatles

Chapter 10

The Legal Implications of Y2K

Y2K Ambulance Chasers

One of the major effects of Y2K will be its legal ramifications. This crisis will certainly create the greatest flood of litigation in history. One software expert suggests the litigation costs will be much higher than the repair costs (which are themselves estimated to be $300 - $600 billion). I have heard a prominent attorney, whose firm is preparing feverishly for the crisis, estimate that there will be a $one trillion Y2K litigation market! Already, many law firms are forming action teams to study the Y2K situation and the money making possibilities it promises for the legal community. If Y2K is, indeed, the single most expensive problem in history, those who suffer its damages will certainly be looking for lawyers. And the lawyers will be searching for victims. Many different kinds of lawsuits can be imagined.

- *Investors whose investments were diminished or even lost will sue the managers or custodians of*

their portfolios. The targets will be banks, stock bro-
kerages, investment counselors, mutual fund man-
agers, etc.

- *Shareholders will sue corporations that did not take*
  adequate or timely action to cure their Y2K prob-
  lems. The target will be publicly traded corporations
  and their directors and officers.

- *Victims and/or their survivors will sue those con-*
  tributing to their injuries or death. Targets will be
  airlines, railroads, hospitals, pharmaceutical compa-
  nies and many others.

- *Individuals and businesses who use computers and*
  software will file class-action lawsuits. The targets
  will be computer and software manufacturers and
  distributors.

- *Businesses whose affairs are impacted by Y2K will*
  sue their vendors for disrupted/ corrupted materials
  and will sue their customers for payment problems.
  The targets will be businesses of all persuasions and
  sizes.

- *Huge lawsuits could erupt over intellectual property*
  rights if the Patent and Trademark Office databases
  become tainted. Also, remember that one of the
  most devastating possible effects of Y2K will be actu-
  al destruction of valid data.

The Real Culprit

Unbelievably, the Year 2000 Problem was first discovered around 1970 when banks and real estate companies

using computers to create amortization tables for 30 year mortgages had trouble getting the last year (2000) to compute correctly. Since then, many far-seeing computer programmers have tried to warn management of the problem. Now the chickens are coming home to roost and the hen house they are flocking to is called management.

Corporate directors and officers have the legal obligation to guard and protect the assets of their companies. Y2K is rapidly becoming a well-known and potentially devastating problem which is certain to occur. Management as a whole has shown an amazing reluctance to deal with the issue however. For many of them, it is now too late. The dam has already broken. Most of these will have the excuse, "We didn't know it was going to be so bad." Management will also be taken to task because their suppliers have Y2K problems. They are supposed to keep track of that sort of thing too. One prominent attorney who specializes in high technology issues says

> *"Failing to fix your upcoming Year 2000 problem ...will expose (companies) to class action law suits, possible loss of coverage from insurance companies, malpractice for professionals, and director and officer liability -- a grand slam!"*
> *Warren S. Reid - WSR Consulting Group*
> *Encino, California*

The bottom line is that management did not cause the Y2K Problem in the first place but their inaction will be judged to be what caused its effects to be so serious. They didn't break the dam but they will be the ones who dawdled and squandered away the response time needed to fix the problem.

The Bean-Counters Too

Annually every publicly owned company must publish a financial statement which includes a written report from the company's management. (If you can call a stock broker and buy stock in a company, it is publicly owned). By law, this management report must identify upcoming events and their expected impact on the company. This financial statement has to be audited by an unbiased accounting firm which then passes judgment on the accuracy of the document.

The Year 2000 is certainly an upcoming event and its expected effects are becoming increasingly well known. Many companies will soon be facing serious Y2K related difficulties. Those who realize the problem soon enough are being forced to take on large costs to fix their problems. Many larger companies are experiencing software repair costs in the tens and even hundreds of millions of dollars. (Prudential Life Insurance for example is budgeting $120 million and Citibank $250 million.)

There are two important issues involved here.

1.   *Are the financial statements of these companies reflecting expected Y2K problems and costs?*

2.   *Are the big accounting firms commenting on Y2K situations in their audits?*

The answer is mostly no. The big accounting firms are getting put into a box because soon they will start taking on liability themselves for not being forthcoming about Y2K. When these two things start happening regularly, it is going to have a terrible effect on the stock market and the lawsuits will start to fly as a result.

Y2K Certification

Formal Y2K Certification is going to become a very big deal. For companies which can become certified, it will be a big bonus and for others who cannot it will be devastating. For a business concern, Y2K Certification means that its products are certified to be date correct. It also means that its computers and software are correct in all their date processing. The time will soon come when the term "Y2K Compliant" or "Y2KOK,"will be as common on products and services as "Made in the U.S.A." Companies able to make this claim will benefit economically as public awareness of Y2K rises. Those companies unable to make this claim will suffer. Contracting is another arena in which Y2K Certification will become very important. Very soon, the federal government (followed by state governments) will require Y2K compliance in all its contracts. It would not be surprising if a national board of Y2K Certification is established. Just what we need.

For example, as this book is being written, the Department of the Navy is considering requiring each contractor doing work for its various agencies to sign a letter certifying Y2K compliance. The language of this requirement reads as follows:

"With regard to Contract number N000XX-XX-C-XXX, please provide your certification, signed by the appropriate corporate officer, that all contract deliverables (both future and already delivered) are Year 2000 compliant. If they are not, please provide a detailed plan outlining what actions you will take to make all contract deliverables Year 2000 compliant, which includes when these actions will be complete and all contract deliverables will be compliant."

I have over thirteen years of government contract work including program management. In my judgment, this is pretty inflammatory stuff and is probably not legally enforceable because it tries to impose this certification ret-roactively. At the very least, it is my prediction this will make great fodder for a multitude of extremely high pro-file lawsuits.

Constitutional Crisis?

The November 1998 general election occurs just after the first set of Y2K spike dates (July 1 and October 1, 1998). The national election will, of course elect members of the House of Representatives plus one third of the members of the Senate. Locally, state legislators, governors and lo-cal officials will be elected and a great multitude of local issues such as bond issues will be voted on.

The primaries for this election cycle will, for the most part, occur prior to the spike dates. One of the things that can happen on spike dates is corruption of databases. For example, data can be accidentally deleted, unknowingly changed or retained when it should be purged. Voter reg-istration records are maintained in databases. These records can be kept either in a single, state-wide database or in a multitude of locally maintained databases. Each will result in its own unique problem. A state might have a single huge problem or a multitude of smaller but dif-fering problems. Either way there will probably be voters who are allowed to vote in one election but not the other. Voter fraud charges will be made. Lawsuits will ensue. The results may or may not be sorted out by the following January when the new legislative bodies are due to be sworn in. Who will the winners be? Who will decide? A severe constitutional crisis could occur at both the state and federal level. Who wins a congressional seat if voter records are unreliable or even lost?

A second type of election problem could happen because most elections themselves are managed by computer. Votes are tabulated and processed electronically by many different methods. This diversity in itself intensifies the problem. What happens in elections if the computers themselves fail? What happens when you can't tell who wins? I suppose the answer is that the election must be processed manually. Has this ever been done as a result of a massive computer failure? Can all types of computerized ballets even be counted manually? I don't know the answer to these questions but I do know Y2K is going raise important constitutional questions in many jurisdictions.

Miscellaneous Effects

The Securities and Exchange Commission (SEC) imposes regulatory reporting requirements on publicly traded corporations. The information is put into government operated databases. This information will likely become corrupted when the associated computers begin malfunctioning. Government efforts to regulate will become ineffective as Y2K approaches.

Warranties are provided to the purchasers of all kinds of products from automobiles to stereo systems. Information concerning who bought what and when is kept in databases by the manufacturing companies. These databases could become inoperative or invalid as Y2K approaches.

Action Steps

Spike Date Precautions

The period of time from a few weeks before a Spike

Date until a few weeks afterwards will be an especially perilous time to undergo any type of legal transaction. Avoid activities such as real estate closings, divorce, marriage, contract signings, major purchases etc. Records of legal transactions will be lost or corrupted. Court dockets will become unreliable. The danger is greatest in local governmental jurisdictions because they are least likely to be able to withstand Y2K problems.

Continuing Precautions

I know I have continued to hammer away at this point but it is one of the most important steps you can take in preparing for the millennium. Maintain hard copies of your legal records including such things as product warranties. Trust nothing to computers. If any piece of information is important to you in any way, get it on paper. Create and use the Y2K Shield.

If you are a business owner, start curing your Y2K difficulties. Learn about Y2K Certification and incorporate it into your marketing plan. If your business has stockholders, keep them informed about your Y2K situation. This is critical to protect yourself from financial negligence or malfeasance lawsuits.

Pressure local election officials to ensure the software used to maintain your voter registration records and to conduct the 1998 elections are Y2K compliant. Chapter 11, What You Can Do To Help, provides details on doing this.

"And now it's up to you,
I think it's only fair"

"She Loves You" - the Beatles

Chapter 11

What You Can Do To Help

Critical Action Step #7 -
Tell Others

This chapter describes specific steps you can take to help your community and the nation itself prepare for the Y2K Crisis and reduce the impact of whatever challenges it brings. If enough people just like you took these steps, the entire country would be better prepared for the difficult times ahead. Helping to create awareness of the problem is the first and foremost of these steps. No problem can be solved until the decision makers admit there is a problem in the first place. Many do not yet believe Y2K is serious although the national press is just now beginning to realize the seriousness of the situation we are facing. It is a natural human tendency to deny problems because dealing with them is usually uncomfortable. This is one of the reasons I am convinced the Y2K Problem will probably not be solved in time to avert great difficulties. People just don't want to admit it is real and too many managers have delayed too long in dealing with the problem. Regardless, we must all do what we can to warn people of the danger so they can prepare for the worst.

How Irritating!

Basically, what I want to show you is how to irritate those managers until you get their attention focused on this issue. Although the Year 2000 Problem manifests itself in technical ways, it is, at its core, a management problem and it must be solved by managers. So that's where we are going to concentrate our awareness efforts. In the government arena, these managers are politicians and bureaucrats. These will be both elected officials and appointed heads of agencies. Within the private sector, you will be exerting your influence on the top management of businesses and other institutions. The key factor in this strategy is to always aim your bullet at the highest target possible. Never deal with an underling when you can figure out how to get to the top guy/gal him/herself.

The Pitch

So how are you going contact these people and what are you going to say to them? Well, I suggest you contact them by mail for reasons which will be apparent momentarily. So that you don't have to draft a letter yourself, a sample is provided in Appendix B which is intended to serve as a generic letter which can be sent to everyone on the list provided below. The generic letter basically says these three things:

1. *It states that you are concerned about the Year 2000 Problem and the effect it could have on you and your family.*

2. *It requests that the recipient provide you with a summary of how he is dealing with the Year 2000 Problem.*

3. *It requests that the recipient sign and return to you an enclosed "Y2K Compliance Certificate."*

This certificate asks for written certification that the goods and services provided to you by the recipient will be free of Y2K related defects and that all databases which contain information about you will be free of Y2K related errors.

The Response

Most people writing a letter to a high ranking government or business official about Y2K would include only points a.) and b.) above. Politicians in particular are used to this kind of letter. The kind that says, "I'm concerned about issue 'A,' what are you going to do about it?" The response to this kind of letter is pretty standard. It goes something like this, "Issue 'A' is very important and I'm concerned about it also and we're doing everything we can about it." Now, you're going to get this kind of response. In fact, most of the responses you get will be just like this.

What's going to be different about your letter and the part of it that is going to be the biggest irritant to the recipients is part 3. They're definitely not going to like this part. Your "Compliance Certificate" is going to be a great worry to them and it will probably end up in the hands of their lawyers. Many of them will ignore this piece of paper and respond just as if they had not even seen the certificate. Many will send the certificate back to you unsigned. A few might even comment on it and give you some sort of cock and bull story why they won't sign it. I would be amazed if you did get back any copies actually signed.

If that's the case, why should you send them this certificate in the first place? The answer is simple. It will get their attention and make them realize they may be liable for something if they don't do their job right. Believe me, when they are faced with the prospect of signing a piece of paper which might make them responsible to you for some sort of damages, they will run for the hills. Regardless of how they respond, you will have achieved your objective which is to force these decision makers to stop and consider that Y2K might be a big problem for them.

Who Gets It?

Here is the list of officials you should write to. I have put an asterisk (*) beside the ones I think are the most critical but I recommend you write to all of them if you can. The generic Y2K letter in Appendix B is constructed so that you can reproduce it and mail it many times over. Mailing addresses for all of the officials at the federal level and many at the state level can be found in Lesko's Info-Power III, book I have mentioned several times previously.

Federal Level

* *President William Clinton*
The White House
1600 Pennsylvania Avenue
Washington DC 20500

* *Vice President Albert Gore*
Old Executive Office Building
Washington DC 20501

(There is a special reason to write to the Vice President. He is the great hi-tech champion in the Clinton administration and will be particularly sensitive to this issue.)

* *U.S. Representative*
* *Both U.S. Senators*
Director, Office of Management and Budget
Administrator, General Services Administration
Secretary of Health and Human Services
Director, Social Security Administration
Secretary of the Treasury
Director, Internal Revenue Service
Director, Federal Deposit Insurance Corporation
Board of Governors, Federal Reserve Board
Director, National Credit Union Administration
Director, Securities and Exchange Commission

State Level

* *Governor*
* *State Representative*
* *State Senator*
State Budget Director
State Tax Authority

County Level

* *County Manager or Administrator*
* *All County Commissioners*
County Tax Authority
County Sheriff

Local Level

* City Manager or Mayor
* Hospital Administrator
* Your employer
Chief of Police
Fire Chief
Superintendent of Schools
School Principals
Colleges and Universities attended
All health care providers

Businesses

* Bank or Credit Union
* Electric Company
* Life insurance provider
* Health insurance provider
Credit Reporting Bureaus
Local Telephone Company
Long Distance Provider
Cable Television Provider
Grocery Store
Pharmacy
Department Store
Water Company
Internet Service Provider
Family Doctor
Family Lawyer
Stockbroker
Pension fund   and all other investment managers
Credit card companies
Mortgage holder
All other creditors

Cats and Dogs

There are other activities you can undertake besides writing letters which could help to spread the word about the Year 2000 Computer Problem. Some of these things follow and I'm certain you could think of others as well.

Tell everybody you know about The Y2K Problem. Articles about the problem are starting to show with some regularity in the press. Y2K has been in newspapers all over the country, it has been covered on CNN and National Public Radio. It has even been in Reader's Digest (October 1996) and in Parade Magazine (September 15, 1996). Most people who have not heard of Y2K will scoff at the idea. One of the best ways to respond to this is to give them a copy of the study which was done in 1996 by the Congressional Research Service (an agency of the Library of Congress). This document is in the public domain so you can copy it all you want. You can also give them a copy of Senator Moynihan's letter to the President about Y2K. It is a real eye-opener. Both of these documents are included in this Survival Guide in Appendix C. Feel free to copy them all you like.

Give copies of this Survival Guide to your family, friends and others in positions of influence in your community such as your pastor, your employer or any of the decision makers listed above. Multiple copies of this Survival Guide can be purchased at a excellent discount. An order form was provided with this Survival Guide.

Go to public meetings of your city council, county commissioners and school board, etc. and force discussions of the Y2K issue. Also do this if your congressman or any other official holds any town-hall type public meetings in your town. At these meetings, you will be met with much skepticism so take along a few copies of Senator Moynihan's letter to the President and the report done by the Congressional Research Service. These two documents should gain you instant credibility.

Write letters to the editors of your local newspapers. See Appendix B for a sample letter. In short, what you can do for your community is to be a nuisance. Talk about the issue and press all the buttons you can reach to make others talk about it as well. Do everything you can to irritate decision makers. Eventually they will have to scratch that itch.

Get into the date awareness habit by inspecting everything for correct date information. Be particularly alert (of course) for the use of two digit years. I have been doing this a lot lately and have even devised sort of a game to go along with my inspection. I watch for two digit years and then point them out to the people using them. I've done this with restaurant bills, supermarket receipts, airline/train tickets and have even mentioned it at my Chiropractor's office. The responses vary from "Huh?" all the way to ordering a copy of this book. Whatever the response, it often gets people thinking about the issue.

"Spread the word and you'll be free."

"The Word" - the Beatles

Chapter 12

Conclusions

Wrap-up

Well, my friend, I have just about said my piece. All that remains is to summarize things and put a final emphasis on a few of the points I consider the most important. I have pulled together a "Y2K Library" of all the books and other materials I recommended throughout this Survival Guide. I have also included information on where to look on the Internet for Y2K information. Finally, I look into the future and speculate on some possible long term effects of Y2K.

Critical Action Steps Redux

Throughout this Survival Guide I have made recommendations to the reader on how to prepare for the Year 2000 Problem. In many chapters I identified specific actions to take or to avoid on or around "Spike Dates" and also continuing precautions to take at all other times. I also identified seven particularly important "Critical Action Steps." These are the most important recommendations in the book. To help pull everything together they are repeated below.

1. *The Y2K Shield* - see Chapter 3. Tells how to obtain
   and protect your most important vital information
   and how to set up a "Vital Information Portfolio."

2. *Buy Lesko's Info Power III* see Chapter 3. This great
   book tells you where information is located and
   how you can get it.

3. *Stay Home* - see Chapter 5. Your home is your castle
   and your fortress against the Year 2000 Crisis.

4. *Store Necessities* - see Chapter 9. Tells how to be
   certain you will always have food, water and other
   vital commodities available for you and your family. This is the ultimate Y2K insurance policy.

5. *Own Gold and Silver Coins* - see Chapter 9. This
   cache of "real money" will ensure you are always
   able   to   carry   on   essential   economic
   transactions.,even if there are no banks or ATM's or
   credit cards in operation.

6. *Move Away From the Big Cities* - see Chapter 9. Get
   off the battlefield and into a small community
   where the dangers of Y2K will be overcome by people who care - your neighbors.

7. *Tell Others* - see Chapter 11. Get out the word. It is
   the best hope we all have to minimize the effects of
   this great catastrophe.

A Y2K Library

I do recommend a small Y2K "library" that will be useful to you as the Year 2000 Crisis picks up steam and

becomes a factor in your life. The list is pretty small and very non-technical. All of these works have been mentioned in previous chapters. Besides my own two contributions to the list, Howard Ruff's book (# 1 below) is the most important. It is twenty years out of date and was written for a different purpose than to prepare the reader for the Y2K Crisis but it is still the finest book of its kind ever written. If you want to be prepared for any bad thing that might happen in the world, this is the book that will help the most.

1. *How to Prosper During the Coming Bad Years, by Howard Ruff. Warner Books, New York, NY, 1979. Probably out of print but can usually be found in used paperback shops for a buck or so.*

2. *Info Power III, by Matthew Lesko. Visible Ink Press, Detroit MI, 1996. Must have! Available at any good bookstore.*

3. *Boy Scout Manual - available from any local store that sells Boy Scouts supplies or by mail from the address shown below.*

   Trading Post
   Albany NY 12205
   Phone 800-734-2721, Fax: 518-869-6439

4. *Making the Best of Basics: Family Preparedness Handbook by James Talmage Stevens. Gold Leaf Press, Carson City NV, 1974. Available at:*

   Lee Dee Stevens
   15123 Little Wren Lane
   San Antonio TX 78255

----

5. *The Coming Race War in America: A Wakeup Call,*
   by Carl Rowan.   Little, Brown and Company, Bos-
   ton, 1996.   Available in any bookstore.

and of course (blush):

6. *A Survival Guide For The Year 2000 Problem.* by
   Jim Lord,   J. Marion Publishing, Bowie MD, 1997
   and its companion:

7. *Jim Lord's Year 2000 Survival Newsletter* J. Marion
   Publishing, Bowie MD, 1997.   Described below.
   Both the Survival Guide and the Survival Newsletter are available using the Order Form at the end
   of this book or by calling, toll-free, 1-888-Y2K-2555.

Surf's Up

The Internet is an incredibly rich source of information about the Year 2000 Problem as well as food storage,
gold and silver coins or any of the other other topics discussed in this Survival Guide. A search of the World
Wide Web using the term 'Y2K," will yield a thousand or
so hits. By all means, plug yourself into this information
flow if you have it available. If not, I strongly recommend
that all readers become computer literate and get plugged
into this incredible resource. Believe me, it is not as difficult as it might seem at first. Nor is it very expensive.
Although there are many sources of information about
Y2K on "the Net," here are some of the key sites all of
which have links to other Y2K sites. If you start with
these you will soon be an expert on the subject. Happy
surfin'.

www.year2000.com

The premier Y2K site operated by Canadian consultant, Peter deJager, who was the first of the Y2K
gurus. Any success the world has in preparing for
the Y2K Crisis will be attributed to Peter's undaunt-
ing efforts.

www.itpolicy.gsa.gov

Operated by the General Services Administration,
this is the most important of the many government
Y2K sites

www.itaa.com

Offered by the Information Technology Association
of America, a prominent trade association and a
leader in making the government aware of Y2K

www.mitre.org

MITRE Corporation, a federally funded research
and development corporation, runs this excellent
site

www.y2ktimebomb.com

This site is a Y2K on-line magazine with terrific,
coverage of what is happening on the Year 2000
scene

www.SurviveY2K.com
By yours truly (re-blush)

Keeping Up

As you read this Survival Guide, it is already out of date. During the time it has taken me to write it, much has happened in a Y2K sense. I expect the pace of change to remain rapid during the whole life of the Y2K Crisis. Many of the developments that take place will be vitally important to you. Additionally, as these changes take place, I will be diligently monitoring the events to evaluate the status of the crisis and to develop new recommendations for my readers on how to react.

To keep my readers up to date on what is happening and what actions they should be taking, I publish a bi-monthly (six times per year) update titled "Jim Lord's Year 2000 Survival Newsletter." It is a close companion and an extension of this Survival Guide and will be published through the entirety of the Year 2000 Problem.

Naturally, I strongly urge you to use this newsletter to plug the gap between the publication of this book and the peak of the crisis. It could provide <u>the critical information</u> you need to weather the storm.

Long Term Effects

Three long term effects of the Year 2000 Problem are discussed in this section. The first will be a healthy skepticism about technology in general and computers in particular. The central questions will be to what extent do we want these devices in our lives and how can we prevent this kind of problem from happening again. Computer software and those who create it will end up with a huge black eye because Y2K is a problem that was completely avoidable. Afterwards, we will understand computer software and its design and engineering as we never have before. Enterprises all over the world will, for the first time, know what software they have and will understand what it does.

As a result of Y2K, a great debate will rage in future years about computers and their place in our society. There will be a much greater reluctance to incorporate new software into our lives and a great hue and cry will rise for exhaustive testing of software before it is allowed into general usage. I would also expect to see software engineers tested and licensed before they are allowed to write computer code intended for public use. In many ways, Y2K will hasten the implementation of the "Information Superhighway" as we discard old, worn out systems and upgrade to more modern equipment and software. In other ways, it will hamper these changes as society pauses to examine more closely where technology is taking us.

Litigation will be the second long term effect. As discussed in Chapter 10, Legal Implications of Y2K, it will go on interminably. In the Year 2010 we will still be embroiled in Y2K lawsuits. Just like we are now up to our necks in liability lawsuits involving injuries from tobacco and breast implants. Y2K will seem to go on forever.

The most serious long term effect of the Year 2000 Crisis will be a pervasive loss of faith in the economic system. Banks, the stock market, insurance companies and the government (at all levels) will never again be trusted by all those who are adults over the time period of the Year 2000 Problem. It will be reminiscent of the distrust of the financial structure of the country by the bank failures and stock market crash of the Great Depression. My expectation is this loss of faith will last for forty years or more.

A Final Thought

My greatest desire is that this book will be <u>useless</u> to you. I hope the dangers I have described over the past several hundred pages are never realized. If that is, indeed, what happens, then you will have taken some precautionary steps unnecessarily.

Here is the good part, however. Those steps will have cost you very little. You will have some food, water and other commodities in storage and you will own some gold and silver coins. I think you should have these things no matter what. They will set your mind at ease about any number of calamities which could strike. If you moved out of the city because of this book, then you will have improved your lifestyle and very likely will have avoided problems which could strike the cities anyway. All in all you will probably be better off.

On the other hand, if the worst of what is possible does occur, this Survival Guide will have served its greatest purpose. Providing you with the means of surviving one of the great catastrophes to strike the modern world - the Year 2000 Catastrophe.

In either case, this book has been created with the desire to help. I hope it does its job. In parting, here is an old sailor's blessing. I wish you ...

"Fair winds and following seas."

Sincerely,

Jim Lord

Appendix A

Technical Details Of Y2K

The Technical Section

The Y2K Problem is not singular but plural in nature. That is, it actually consists of a number of date related problems. For this reason, it is sometimes referred to as the Y2K Family of Problems. Some of these stand on their own merit and some are derivative in nature. For example, the two-digit year problem can manifest itself in several different ways, each of which is caused by the two-digit year shortcut. Several of these are covered below. One of the many factors that leads to the stunning complexity of the Y2K Problem is that it extends to so many facets of computers. In this regard, it is somewhat like cancer, which is a family of related diseases capable of striking many different body organs from the brain to the blood to the bladder. Y2K can affect, for example, operating systems, application software, data, software development tools, compilers, networking software, utilities and even some hardware. Some critics believe Y2K will affect only old, main-frame computing systems. Nothing could be further from the truth. New desktop systems are being sold today which will fail on January 1, 2000.

The Y2K Problem is sometimes characterized as being similar to a computer virus. It has even been called the "Mother of All Viruses." In many ways, Y2K does behave in this fashion but this terminology sort of implies that Y2K is something that you can passively "catch" if you are unlucky or careless and this is not the case. Peter deJager, a well known consultant, who was an "early adopter" of the Y2K Crisis and who has testified about the problem to the U.S. Congress, refers to Y2K as a "genetic defect" in that the problem was designed in from the start and has been there all along just resting away in our machines waiting for the right time and conditions to strike. Both of these medical analogies have some merit. Whichever is the more accurate, Y2K will certainly be the most wide-spread and well-known technical "disease" in history. (Mad Computer Disease?)

The following discussion, which is in no particular or-der or priority explains some of these individual "cancers."

Two Digit Years. This is by far the most widely known type of Year 2000 Problem partly because it is so common and partly because it is easy for the non-technical sort of person to understand. It is a problem that shows up in many older software applications but can be found in very recent software as well. The fundamental problem results when the Year 2000 is erroneously interpreted as the year zero. It leads to several different types of computational errors. An example might be a program which needs to calculate a persons age in years based on the current year and the person's year of birth. Lets say we need the age of a person who was born in the year 1914. Shown below are two calculations, one based on the current year of 1996 and the second based on a current year of 2000 (obtained from the computer's system clock of course).

Actual current year	1996	2000
Two digit current year	96	00
Minus year of birth	- 14	- 14
Age	82	- 14

Most age calculations will disregard the sign of a number since "everyone" knows a person can't be a negative number of years old so this elderly person's age is now recorded in error as 14 years. Although some eighty-two year olds might like to be fourteen again, some computer programs will now decide this person is ineligible for Social Security benefits and Medicaid, can't possess a driver's license, can't vote, is a truant if not registered in the public school system, can't purchase alcohol, tobacco or Playboy magazines and can't get into an R-rated movie but could be admitted to the pediatrics ward at the local hospital. I admit to some silliness in this example but it is easy to see how date-related calculations using two digits years could produce some pretty disastrous results.

Forced "19XX". Many computer applications and some computer chips process the year using only the last two digits and then just stick the two digits "19" in front of the result. It makes the answer look OK, but the processing taking place beforehand will suffer the same two digit errors pointed out above.

System Clock Rollover. All modern computers maintain an internal electronic clock which is powered by a small battery even when the computer is turned off or unplugged. This internal clock is called the "system clock," because it is provided as one of the features of the computer's operating system (O/S). The system clock maintains the date and day of the week as well as the time. When the Year 2000 arrives, the system clock on many computers will fail to accurately "roll over" to the new year. In fact, this is sometimes called the "odometer problem," and manifests itself differently depending on the make of the computer. Computers using the very popular Microsoft DOS operating system will roll over to either 1980 or 1984 depending on the computer hardware (see hardware problems below). The later Microsoft Windows O/S (currently the most widely used personal computer O/S in the world) rolls over to the year 1900.

In and of itself, this is not much of a problem but its derivatives are devastating. Many computer applications have instructions to "go get today's date from the system clock" and use the result in some calculation. I discuss these derivative problems in other sections in this Appendix.

It's easy to test your computer to see if it has a Y2K system clock roll-over problem. Just set your computer's clock ahead to 11:55 P.M. on December 31, 1999. Turn the computer off and wait at least five minutes then turn the computer back on again. If the clock indicates the correct date your O/S is OK. Please note the warning below before conducting this test. Also, be sure to return the clock back to the current day afterwards.

Unexpected Leap Year. The Year 2000 is a Leap Year but most computer programmers think it is not and many computer applications will not treat it as such. There are three rules for determining if any given year is a Leap Year. These rules are explained below.

a. Years divisible by 4 are Leap Years. By this rule, the Year 2000 is a Leap Year.

b. The exception to this rule is that years divisible by 100 are not Leap Years. By this exception, therefore, the Year 2000 is not a leap Year. Most computer programmers (and other people as well) are aware of this rule.

c. The exception to this exception is that years divisible by 400 are Leap Years. By this exception, of course, the year 2000 is once again a Leap Year. Most people, including many computer programmers, are not aware of this rule.

So, by the above rules, the Year 2000 ends up being what I call an Unexpected Leap Year which many computer programs do not take into account. This problem is also easy to detect. Use the same technique as described above in the system clock section but set the clock to 11:55 P.M. on February 28, 2000 and see what happens. If the date afterwards is something other than February 29, your O/S is faulty. Be sure to check the next several days in the date sequence as well. In some operating systems, February 29th occurs correctly but the day after that is February 29th also. Be sure to return the clock back to the current day after the test.

WARNING ! !

Do not open applications or documents while conducting either of these two tests. Doing so could PERMANENTLY corrupt your data.

Just as an aside, February 29, 1996, which was an Ex-pected Leap Year, still caused problems for some computer systems. The state of Arizona's lottery computer, for example, failed on that day and the state lost the day's income. Additionally, in Sweden, cellular telephone services were disrupted country-wide due to a Leap Year related computer software problem.

False End of File. In most database programs, the applications software and the data itself are maintained as separate files. When the application file needs a piece of data it retrieves it from the database file which is usually stored on a hard drive or on magnetic tape. Virtually all of the massive mainframe databases work this way. To save space in memory or to reduce data entry time, the year has commonly been represented using only two digits. Inside these huge databases, computer programmers needed some way to tell the computer when it had reached the end of the data. This is especially important when the application is conducting either find or sort operations. A "find" operation might be something like, "Find everyone born in 1955." A sort operation might be "List everybody in alphabetical order." Finds and sorts are two of the more common types of database operations performed. To do either of these the computer needs to be able to locate the End of the File (or EOF) so it will know how far to look.

Now here is the bad part. For many years, in databases with two digit years, computer programmers have used the two digits "99" to identify the EOF point in the data. As a result, when actual "99" data is entered into the database, inaccurate sorts and finds will start to occur because the computer will think the actual data is the End of the File, hence the term "False EOF". "99" in a database field is also commonly used as a "trigger" to cause the application program to take all kinds of programming actions such as purging records and other equally unpleasant things. Programmers used this convention because they didn't think these databases would still be around come 1999 so why worry. This will be a major part of the Year 2000 problem especially in the government sector because they maintain some of the oldest and largest databases in existence. such as those used by the Social Security Administration and the Internal Revenue Service. It is also serious because these problems start showing up as early as July 1, 1998 (Fiscal Year turnover for 46 states), a full year and a half before the "00" types of problems, leaving much less time to fix the problem. As mentioned in Chapter 2, 1999 will be a very, very ugly year and includes four of the major Spike Dates.

The experts in repairing the Y2K Problem in computers agree the repair efforts in a given system should be completed a full year in advance of when the problem is expected to first start appearing. This means New York State (whose fiscal year turns over to "99" on April 1, 1998) should have all "Year 99" susceptible systems completely repaired by April 1, 1997. July 1, 1998 had the key date for forty-six other states.

Importation of "Tainted" Data. The most important trend taking place in the computing world today is the extensive networking taking place. Although the Internet is the most prominent feature of this trend, it is probably not the most important aspect from a Y2K perspective. That spot belongs to the worldwide proliferation of the business and government networks known as Local Area Networks (LAN's) and Wide Area Networks (WAN's). These connections allow multiple computers to be tied together in what are essentially permanent data pipelines.

The Y2K implications of these networks is that even if one computer and its software and its data are "cleansed" of Y2K errors, it can become recontaminated by importing "tainted" data from another computer that has not become scrubbed. One common way to clean up two digit year data, for example, is to expand the year field to four digits and then expand all the year data out to four digits. In other words, convert all those bad two digit "96's" to good, four digit "1996's". Now, however, nothing prevents year data from outside sources containing only two digit years from being imported into those four digit fields. Obviously if there is room in the database field for four digits, there is also room for two digit data and you can't tell when this "tainted" stuff arrives.

Here's an example. General Motors uses over 500 vendors, virtually all of whom are tied directly into GM's main computer system so that their business processes are completely automated. Great for efficiency but a potential disaster if they start swapping bad data. Most very large retailers and manufacturers (such as the Wal-Marts and the Sear's) use this kind of networking arrangement between themselves and their vendors.

Hidden Dates.   Many inventory applications hide a two digit year inside a serial number. Later on, the application will extract the date out and use it within a processing algorithm. For example, a serial number format might look something like:

425923362

It is impossible by inspection to realize that the "92" buried inside this number actually represents the year of manufacture of the item. Many consulting companies specializing in Y2K software repair use specialized tools

which inspect computer code and data looking for instances of two digit years. As you can imagine, these tools
would be useless for data constructed in this fashion. This
is one of the most vexing and dangerous Y2K problems
because it is invisible and is extremely difficult to find and
fix. Imagine for a moment a computer used to operate a
nuclear waste management facility. Now imagine all
those barrels of horribly toxic waste with all those bar coded serial numbers on them constructed like the example
above. And then think of a computer program that helps
to make decisions about when that waste is to be treated or
buried or transferred or whatever. Pretty scary, huh?

<u>Embedded Processing.</u> Many computing systems use
firmware rather than software, meaning that the computerized instructions are permanently embedded into a
computer chip and cannot be changed like software can.
To change firmware, one must dismantle the equipment
and replace the computer chip containing the coded instructions. The extent of embedded processing is truly
amazing in today's modern world. Many consumer goods
such as automobiles, microwave ovens, VCR's, cellular
phones, pagers and even talking toys and greeting cards
use embedded processors. Any of these devices which
make date-related calculations are prone to Y2K problems.
     The most serious worry about embedded processors
with date calculation problems is military systems. Satellites are the biggest concern because it is not possible, of
course, to put them in the repair shop to replace a computer chip. Other systems to be concerned about but
which can be repaired (at great expense, of course) are
weapons such as missiles and "smart" bombs, RADAR,
communications and navigations systems.

Here is one example. (To be precise, this example is not technically a Y2K problem, it is a date-related problem that occurs, coincidentally, very near the Year 2000.) The Global Positioning System (GPS) consists of 24 satellites positioned around the earth in orbits such that several satellites are always within a direct line of sight from any point on the surface of the globe. These satellites broadcast time and position information which can be received by a special radio (called a GPS Receiver) which contains an embedded processor. By comparing the signals from several satellites at once, the processor is able to establish the GPS Receiver's longitude and latitude with a high degree of accuracy. GPS is an extremely important technology which received very high marks after its extensive and highly successful use in the Persian Gulf War. Briefly stated, it gave our military forces the ability to determine their position with great accuracy at all times and in all conditions. GPS receivers are now also installed in a wide range of military systems.

GPS has also become a vital technology commercially in such industries as shipping, agriculture, trucking and fishing and in consumer use by boater, hikers, campers, fishermen etc. In the past five years, millions of GPS Receivers have been sold commercially worldwide.

Now here's the crunch. It has only been recently recognized that GPS Receivers have a date rollover problem. At midnight August 21-22, 1999, the GPS system clock rolls over and the date becomes January 6, 1980. Since GPS is a satellite-based system and satellites depend on accurate date and time information in order to determine their position with accuracy, all GPS Receivers will at that point begin giving wildly inaccurate locations. In other words, that hiker up in the Rockies will suddenly be told by his GPS Receiver that he is in Paris or Ethiopia. Virtually all GPS Receivers in the world will have to be recalled in order to install a new computer chip. I would suppose that some GPS manufacturers will simply go out of business before then rather than face this cost. This is a big, big problem and since GPS is first and foremost a military system, this fiasco will end up being a major embarrassment to the government and a potentially huge cost as the manufacturer's lawsuits start to fly.

Amateur Programmers. One scary aspect of Y2K is the completely unknown and unknowable danger posed by amateur programmers. Over the past ten years or so the power of personal computers and inexpensive, commercial software has reached amazing plateaus. The $2,500 computer this Survival Guide is being written on is vastly more powerful in all aspects than the huge, million dollar mainframe computer I used in my college days 23 years ago. Many software packages give the user wonderful capabilities to create executable software. Wonderfully useful and versatile tools can be produced using spreadsheet and database programs costing just a few hundred dollars. The result is that trained software professionals are no longer required to create very useful custom software. Amateur programmers have the capability to produce it on their own.

The danger is that virtually none of this software has the underlying engineering infrastructure which provides configuration control, testing, analysis, and, most importantly, quality assurance. This is all just a fancy way of saying that nobody really knows what the hell is out there. There is a lot of it, however, and thousands of businesses from the single guy running a little home business to the largest corporations are dependent on it in totally unknown ways. I don't know what kind of Y2K related problems will result from amateur programmers. But it is sure going to be interesting finding out.

"Try to see it my way,
do I have to keep on talking till I can't go on?"

"Try to See it My Way" - the Beatles

Appendix B

Sample Letters

There are two aspects to preparing for the Year 2000 Problem, preparing yourself and your family for whatever might happen and trying to influence others to take action. This Appendix is designed to give you some assistance in the second of those tasks. Following, you will find sample letters you can use to help "irritate" and hopefully spur into action those who control enterprises in Y2K jeopardy. These sample letters are as follows:

FOIA Request. The Freedom of Information Act (FOIA) gives you the right to obtain any information held by the federal government that is not classified for national security purposes. Some states have similar laws. This letter shows you how to use this law to request any information.

Letter to a decision maker. Recipients of this letter fall into two groups but this letter that can be used for both groups, The first group is public officials (congressmen, mayors, school board members etc.). These politicians usually treat letters from the public very seriously. Since most government agencies are ill prepared for the Y2K

Problem, the best way to get these officials off their duffs is to pester them with letters. If they receive enough letters they will take notice.

The second group includes leaders of business and non-profit enterprise such as banks, stock brokers, hospitals, churches and retail outlets. Unlike politicians, these decision makers don't receive very many letters from the public. Accordingly, they may be quicker to agitate.

Be sure to include a Y2K Compliance Certificate with each letter. It'll bug the very dickens out of them.

Y2K Compliance Certificate. Include this document in letters to both types of decision makers. It is designed to get their attention and force the issue. Even if they ignore it, you will make them think.

Letter to the editor of a newspaper. This letter is designed to be read by the public. As you will see, it is just a slightly modified version of the previous letter. Hopefully it will raise public awareness of Y2K and intrigue readers enough to investigate the issue further.

All of the letters in this appendix are provided for your convenience. You are free to modify them and to use them in any way you desire. This type of inexpensive public relations campaign is the strongest weapon you have in helping your community prepare for the Y2K Crisis.

Good Luck.

Note: In my work as a government contractor, I have used FOIA requests to obtain contracting information from a number of government agencies. I found the process to be highly effective and was uniformly pleased with the response I received from the agencies involved. They were consistently courteous and prompt in handling my requests. The following page shows you what a FOIA request might look like:

Date

Freedom of Information Officer
Name of Agency
Address of Agency
City, State, Zip

Re: Freedom of Information Act Request

Dear Sir:

This is a request under the Freedom of Information Act.

I request that a copy of the following documents be provided to me (identify the documents or information desired as fully as possible).

In order to determine my status to assess fees you should know that I am an individual seeking information for my personal use and not for any commercial purposes.

(Optional Paragraph) I am willing to pay fees for this request up to a maximum of $(insert amount). If you estimate that the fees will exceed this amount please inform me first.

Thank you for your consideration of this request.

Sincerely,

Name
Address

Re: Year 2000 Computer Crisis

Dear Decision Maker:

I am deeply concerned about your response to the Year 2000 Computer Crisis (sometimes called the "**Millennium Time Bomb**.")

This problem occurs when computers which use two-digit years will misinterpret the year 2000 to be "00" or zero. Computers infected with this "bug" will either shut down or produce errors in date calculations. This problem is alarmingly pervasive and affects many systems in current use.

Experts believe global repair costs could exceed **One Trillion Dollars**. Failure to undertake these repairs, however, could result in:

- the failure of government to collect revenues; provide vital services or disburse entitlements, pensions, employee salaries, contract payments and interest due on government securities,

• the inability of banks, stock exchanges, investment firms and insurance companies to process and track financial transactions,

• the bankruptcy of thousands of businesses and non-profit enterprises as they lose the ability to purchase materials; make payroll; receive and process income; pay obligations or deliver products or services to the marketplace,

• the widespread breakdown of infrastructure components such as water; electric power; telephone service; building access, elevator and air-conditioning systems and even traffic control systems.

The Year 2000 Crisis is the most serious technical problem the world has ever faced. If decisive action is not taken immediately, an economic disaster of catastrophic proportions could ensue.

I respectfully request that you inform me of actions you are taking to address the Year 2000 Crisis. Additionally, I ask that you endorse and return to me the enclosed "Year 2000 Certification Certificate."

Your consideration in this critical matter is greatly appreciated.

Sincerely:

Name
Address

Y2K Compliance Certificate

The Year 2000 (Y2K) Problem occurs when computers which use two-digit years misinterpret the year 2000 to be "00" or zero.   Computers infected with this "bug" will either shut down or produce errors in date calculations. The Year 2000 Crisis is the most serious and the most expensive technical problem the world has ever faced.

Failure to undertake repairs to these computer systems could result in:

- the extensive disruption of vital government services and programs,

- the inability of financial institutions to accurately process transactions,

- the bankruptcy of thousands of businesses and non-profit enterprises, and

- the widespread breakdown of critical public services and utilities.

By my signature below, I certify that I am aware of the nature, the severity and the time criticality of the Year 2000 Computer Problem. I hereby pledge my commitment to ensuring the delivery of goods and services to the public which are free of date related, Y2K defects.

Signed_____   Date_____

Dear Editor:

The following is submitted for inclusion in your publication.

"I am deeply concerned about the response of government officials and business leaders to the Year 2000 Computer Crisis (sometimes called the "**Millennium Time Bomb**.")

Computers which use two-digit years will misinterpret the year 2000 to be "00" or zero. Computers infected with this "bug" will either shut down or produce errors in date calculations.   This problem is alarmingly pervasive and affects many systems in current use.

Experts believe global repair costs could exceed **One Trillion Dollars.** Failure to undertake these repairs, however, could result in:

- the failure of government to collect revenues; provide vital services or disburse entitlements, pensions, employee salaries, contract payments and interest due on government securities,

- the inability of banks, stock exchanges, investment firms and insurance companies to process and track financial transactions,

- the bankruptcy of thousands of businesses and non-profit enterprises as they lose the ability to purchase materials; make payroll; receive and process income; pay obligations or deliver products or services to the marketplace,

- the widespread breakdown of infrastructure components such as water; electric power; telephone service; building access, elevator and air-conditioning systems and even traffic control systems.

The Year 2000 Crisis is the most serious technical problem the world has ever faced. If decisive action is not taken immediately, an economic disaster of catastrophic proportions could ensue. Your support in the dissemination of this information is greatly appreciated."

Thank you for your consideration.

Sincerely:

Name
Address

*"It took me so, long, to find out,
and I found out."*

"Day Tripper" - the Beatles

Appendix C

Y2K Source
Materials

This Appendix contains Y2K material from other published sources. The material includes the following:

1. *A letter to President Bill Clinton written by Daniel P Moynihan, Democratic Senator from the state of New York. The letter was published in the official congressional record. on August 11, 1996*

2. *A report from the Congressional Research Service (CRS) which conducted a study on the Year 2000 Computer Problem at the request of Senator Moynihan. The CRS is a branch of the Library of Congress.*

Since these documents are in the public domain you may make unlimited copies of them and distribute or even sell them at will.

U.S. Senate, Washington, D.C.
July 31, 1996

The President,
The White House,
Washington, D.C.

Dear Mr. President:

I hope this letter reaches you. I write to alert you to a problem which could have extreme negative economic consequences during your second term. The "Year 2000 Time Bomb." This has to do with the transition of computer programs from the 20th to the 21st century.

The main computer languages from the '50's and '60's such as COBOL, FORTRAN, and Assembler were designed to minimize consumption of computer memory by employing date fields providing for only six digits. The date of this letter in "computerese," for example, is 96-07-31, The century designation "19" is assumed.

The problem is that many computer programs will read January 1, 2000 as January 1, 1900. Computer programs will not recognize the 21st century without a massive rewriting of computer codes.

I first learned of all this in February and requested a study by the Congressional Research Service. The study, just now completed, substantiates the worst fears of the doomsayers. (A copy of the CRS study is attached.) The Year 2000 problem ("Y2K") is worldwide. Each line of computer code needs to be analyzed and either passed on or be rewritten. The banking system is particularly vulnerable. A money center bank may have 500 million lines of code to be revised at a cost of $1 per line. That's a $500 million problem. (I learn from Lanny Davis that his client, the Mars Company, estimates the cost of becoming

Y2K date compliant at $100 million to $200 million. Mars is only a candy company.) One would expect that a quick fix of the problem would have been found but it hasn't happened and the experts tell me it is not likely.

There are three issues. First, the cost of reviewing and rewriting codes for Federal and state governments which will range in the billions of dollars over the next three years. Second, the question of whether there is time enough to get the job done and, if not, what sort of triage we may need. I am particularly concerned about the IRS and Social Security in this respect. Third, the question of what happens to the economy if the problem is not resolved by mid-1999? Are corporations and consumers not likely to withhold spending decisions and possibly even withdraw funds from banks if they fear the economy is facing chaos?

I have a recommendation. A Presidential aide should be appointed to take responsibility for assuring that all Federal agencies including the military be Y2K date compliant by January 1, 1999 and that all commercial and industrial firms do business with the Federal government also be compliant by that date. I am advised that the Pentagon is further ahead on the curve here than any of the Federal agencies. You may wish to turn to the military to take command of dealing with the problem

The computer has been a blessing; if we don't act quickly, however, it could become the curse of the age.

Respectfully,

Daniel Patrick Moynihan

The Year 2000

Computer Challenge

A

Report Conducted by

The Congressional
Research Service

June, 1996

The Year 2000 Computer Challenge

SUMMARY

Most computer systems in use today can only record dates in a two-digit format for the year. Under this system, computers will fail to operate properly when years after 1999 are used, because the year 2000 is indistinguishable from 1900. This problem could have a serious impact on a wide range of activities that use computers. Information systems must be inspected, and modified, if necessary, before January 1, 2000 to avoid major system malfunctions.

Many managers initially doubted the seriousness of this problem, assuming that an easy technical fix would be developed. Several independent research firms, however, have refuted this view, with the conclusion that inspecting all computer systems and converting date fields where necessary and then testing modified software will be a very time-consuming and costly task. Research firms predict that due to a lack of time and resources, the majority of US businesses and government agencies will likely not fix all of their computer systems before the start of the new millennium.

Most agencies and businesses have come to understand the difficulties involved, although some have not yet started implementing changes. Several companies have emerged offering services to work on year-2000 conversion, and software analysis product are commercially available to assist with finding and converting flawed software code. Even with the assistance of these products, however, most of the work will still have to be done by humans.

Federal agencies are generally aware of the year-2000 challenge and most are working to correct it. Agencies that manage vast databases, conduct massive monetary transactions, or interact extensively with other computer systems, face the greatest challenge. An interagency committee has been established to raise awareness of the year-2000 challenge and facilitate federal efforts at solving it. The interagency committee has initiated several actions, such as requiring vendor software listed in future federal procurement schedules to be year-2000 compliant and specifying four digit year fields for federal computers. The shortage of time to complete year-2000 computer changes may force agencies to prioritize their systems. Agencies may also need to shift resources from other projects to work on year-2000 efforts. State and local governments, as well as foreign organizations, will also have significant year-2000 conversion problems.

Congressional hearings have been held recently to investigate the year-2000 challenge, and a legislative provision was introduced directing the Defense Department to assess the risk to its systems resulting from it. Several options exist for congressional consideration. One option is to provide special funding to federal agencies for year-2000 conversion. While agencies are reluctant to request additional funds, some observers contend this may be necessary. Another option is to give agencies increased autonomy in reprogramming appropriated funds for year-2000 efforts. A third, less controversial alternative is to continue to raise public awareness through hearings and by overseeing federal efforts.

CONTENTS

DESCRIPTION OF THE PROBLEM/CHALLENGE

SHOULD WE BE CONCERNED?

STRATEGIES FOR CORRECTING THE PROBLEM

STATUS OF FEDERAL AGENCY EFFORTS

Interagency Committee
Issues for Federal Agencies

STATUS OF STATE GOVERNMENTS, PRIVATE SECTOR AND FOREIGN GOVERNMENT EFFORTS

CONGRESSIONAL ACTIVITY

ISSUES AND OPTIONS FOR CONGRESS

Is the Problem Serious Enough to Warrant Congressional Action?
What Are the Options for Congressional Action?
More Funding
Reprogramming Funds
Continued Oversight
Standards Issues
International Issues
The future

The Year 2000 Computer Challenge

DESCRIPTION OF THE PROBLEM/CHALLENGE

Most computer systems in use today record dates in a format using a two digit number for the year; for example, 96 represents the year 1996. The two digit year field is very common among older systems, designed when memory storage was more expensive, but is also used in many systems built today. With this format, however, the year 2000 is indistinguishable from 1900. The year data field in computer programs performs various functions, such as calculating age, sorting information by date, or comparing multiple dates. Thus, when years beyond 1999 are entered under this format, computer systems will fail to operate properly. Given society's increasing reliance on computers, this problem could have a significant impact on a wider range of activities and interests worldwide, including commerce, government operations, military readiness, and the overall economy.

Computer systems of all sizes (mainframe, mini, and micro) as well as local area network and telecommunication systems must be assessed for this problem and converted to a four digit year field where necessary. Year data fields must be corrected in operating systems, compilers, applications, procedures, and databases. Unfortunately, it is often impossible to determine whether and how a computer system needs to be modified without reviewing all of its software code. While correcting the problem for stand-alone PC's may not be difficult, experts agree that all computer systems need to be inspected, corrected and tested before the start of the next millennium, January 1, 2000, to avoid mayor system malfunctions.

SHOULD WE BE CONCERNED?

Research conducted by several independent consulting firms concludes that the problem is formidable. The Gartner Group, an information technology research firm, estimates that it may cost $30 billion to correct the problem in government computers systems of the federal agencies and up to $600 billion worldwide. This is based on an estimated average cost of $1.10 per line of software code. Other independent research firms, including IDC Government (an information technology consulting firm) and the Mitre Corporation (a Federally Funded Research and Development Center), do not dispute this estimate. (See Note 1)

While correcting the year field is technically simple, the process of analyzing, correcting, testing, and integrating software and hardware among all computer systems that must interact is a very complex management task. In most cases, it is too expensive to rewrite software code for the entire system. The overall task is made more difficult by the plethora of computer languages in existence today, the lack of source code and documentation for older software, and the shortage of programmers with skills in older languages. As a further complication, the year 2000 is a special leap year that only occurs every 400 years to keep the calendar accurate. Many software products will not account for the extra day needed in the year 2000.

Many business managers initially doubted the seriousness of this problem, assuming that an easy technical fix would be developed. Others suspect the software services industry was overstating the problem to sell their products and services. For example, the Information Technology Association of America (ITAA), which represents the software and information services industry, has stated that for all US. computing systems, estimates for fixing the year field range between $50 and $75 billion. Some wonder whether ITAA could be exaggerating the problem to bolster the demand for consulting services of its member companies. Some question the objectivity of the cost estimates from other research firms, since these firms are providing services for year 2000 conversion. One critic suggests that because this is one of the few software problems that lay people can understand it is easy for software service providers to generate concern among managers and obtain additional resources for software maintenance. (See note 2)

After investigating the problem, however, many computer scientists, programmers, and more recently, their managers, appear to have assessed the magnitude of the problem, and the resources and time necessary to correct it, as formidable. Most agencies and businesses are convinced that this issue warrants executive-level attention. They point to specific problems that have already occurred and numerous others that will occur if it is not fixed. All vulnerable computer systems must be fixed by January 1, 2000 to avoid widespread erroneous automatic transactions that could be irreparable. Some programs that work with future dates may encounter problems before the next millennium. Others have already had problems. Some potential consequences of failing to convert systems using a two-digit year are listed below.

* The Social Security Administration would miscalculate the age of citizens, causing payments to be sent to people who are not eligible for benefits while those who should be eligible would not receive their payments.

* The Internal Revenue Service would miscalculate the standard deduction on its income tax returns for persons over age 65, causing incorrect records of revenues

and payments due.

   * Certain Defense Department weapons systems could fail to function properly if used during or after the turn of the century.

   * The Federal Aviation Administration's air traffic controllers could generate erroneous flight schedules that may misguide aircraft or cause takeoff or landing conflicts.

   * State and local computer systems could become corrupted with false records, causing errors in income and property tax records, payroll, retirement systems, motor vehicle registration, utilities regulation, and a breakdown of some public transportation systems.

   * The banking industry's schedules for various loans and mortgages could be erroneously updated after the year 2000.

   * Securities firms and insurance companies could produce erroneous records of stock transactions or insurance premiums.

   * Telephone companies (both long distance and local) could record dates incorrectly, causing errors in consumer's bills or a lapse in service.

   * Credit cards with expiration dates after the year 2000 could fail the credit check that is routinely performed when a purchase is made.

   * Data on pharmaceutical drugs with expiration dates after the year 2000 would indicate that the medication is expired.

*   Medical records could become corrupted leading to improper treatment of patients.

*   Businesses of all types and sizes may make errors in their planning, budget, accounts receivable, purchasing, accounts payable, revenue, pension/loan forecasts, payroll, garnishments, material supplies and inventories.

STRATEGIES FOR CORRECTING THE PROBLEM

Software analysis tools can be useful to assess the extent of the problem for specific cases. Software tools are commercially available to assist with the conversion of year fields to four digits. Various tools can identify locations in software code where date references occur, make the necessary changes, and test the upgraded system. Testing is particularly laborious because the modified software must be tested in conjunction with all possible combinations of other software programs it interacts with to ensure functioning has not changed. There may not be enough time, however, for in-house personnel at many agencies to purchase a software analysis tool, learn how to use it, and perform the software conversion and testing. According to one estimate, these tools can only reduce the human work-time by 20-30% at most. (See note 3) Furthermore, sharing analysis tools in most circumstances is prohibited under copyright laws.

Another consideration is whether to use contractor support, in-house personnel, or some mix of the two. Several companies have emerged offering services to work on year-2000 conversion. Many businesses and government agencies may be able to address the problem more efficiently and effectively by hiring experienced contractors. (See note 4). Unfortunately, many of the firms that specialize in year-2000 conversion are already under contract with the larger Private Sector corporations. If in-house staff have an in depth understanding of the software, the company may be better off working on the conversion internally. In many cases, a combination of in-house and contractor support will be used.

Several other technical issues must be considered. Many experts say that software should be analyzed, and modified if necessary, before the start of 1999, to leave ample time to test and debug the system while running in parallel with the existing system. This would leave only two and a half years to complete the conversion process. In some cases, the problem can be fixed without having to add two more digits to the year field. For example, in some cases where the date is printed rather than used for further calculations, the number 19 can be replaced by 20 in front of the two digit year for years after 1999. This would be easier than converting to a four digit year field, and would work until the year 2100, when new computer technology should be in use. Most computer functions that calculate an age or compares two different ages will likely require changing the year field to four digits.

Another major concern is that even if a company or government agency corrects the problem within its own system, it may need to interact with other computer systems. Other systems that are not year-2000 compliant could send file information into the corrected databases, corrupting those databases. Flawed data can easily enter from the private sector into government agencies' database, and from foreign countries into US computer system.

While the technology exists to address the problem, the two main constraints in the year-2000 challenge are funding and time. Because of the skepticism over the seriousness of the problem, computer programmers have had difficulty convincing their managers that resources should be put into this effort. The extra time to generate awareness at all levels in organizations has led to procrastination and delays in starting the work. Some of the blame can also be assessed to the programmers and software companies that did not use four digit year fields in their products. Correcting the year-2000 problem will prevent companies from making costly errors or going out of business but will not contribute to increased productivity or enable a business to provide any new service. In addition, for some organizations, analyzing, compiling, and testing the software will require more computer resources than are currently available without interrupting normal production. Companies may well experience substantial opportunity costs resulting from the need to use resources originally planned for other software projects.

STATUS OF FEDERAL AGENCY EFFORTS

The information resources management personnel at most federal agencies are aware of the problem and are beginning to take corrective action. The Social Security Administration (SSA) identified the problem in 1989 and is the furthest along among federal agencies. SSA plans to complete and test all software changes by December 31, 1998, and run the corrected software in production one full year before 2000.

The Department of Defense (DOD) has more recently become involved with the year-2000 challenge, with different DOD organizations at various phases of solving it. While DOD's finance community began to address the problem in 1991, for many DOD systems the work has not yet begun. A major problem for DOD is managing the efforts across all of the services and defense agencies to maximize efficiency and coordinate chances among system that interact across organizations. DOD has adopted a decentralized approach, letting each service and defense agency determine how to best solve its own year-2000 issues. The DOD coordinator is the Principal Director for Information Management under the Assistant Secretary for Command, Control, Communications, and Intelligence, in the Office of Secretary of Defense. This office, assisted by the Defense Information Systems Agency, serves to promote awareness, facilitate sharing of information, and avoid duplication within DOD (See note 6)

DOD has several unique concerns apart from other Federal agencies, For example hardware changes must be made in some weapon systems whose clocks store dates using two-digit codes. Computer chips that store dates in "firmware" may have to be replaced on missiles and other weapon components. Some of those chips,, however, may no longer be in production. In addition, DOD has many unusual computer languages for which software analysis tools are not commercially available. Given the limited time and resources, DOD is focusing on correcting its mission critical systems, and may use temporary fixes for other systems.

Many other federal departments and agencies face a major challenge in making their computer systems year-2000 compliant to insure the safe and continuous operations of the federal government. The Department of Treasury oversees the massive databases of the Internal Revenue Service, Customs; and Bureau of Alcohol, Tobacco and Firearms. (See note 7) Other agencies with enormous task of correcting their computer systems include the Veteran's Administration, the Department of Transportation (which oversees the Federal Aviation Administration), the Department of Justice (overseeing the Federal Bureau of Investigation), and the Administrative Office of the US Courts.

Interagency Committee

Last year, the Office of Management and Budget (OMB) asked SSA to lead interagency discussions to raise awareness of the year-2000 challenge. As a result, SSA assembled an interagency ad hoc committee to facilitate the efforts of federal agencies. SSA has held several meetings with other federal agencies to help educate staff about the issue, and provide a forum to share cross-cutting ideas and strategies. Attendance at these meetings was initially small, but has increased to over 30 participating agencies. SSA emphasizes that the agencies that own the software are responsible for correcting it, and that the interagency committee can only facilitate their efforts.

The interagency committee has made some progress toward helping Federal agencies deal with the problem. With committee prompting, the General Services Administration (GSA) will require all vendor software listed in future GSA procurement schedules to be year-2000 compliant. The interagency committee is developing a precise definition of year-2000 compliance for GSA to use in future schedules. Due to contractual obligations with vendors, GSA is unable to place new requirements for year 2000 compliance on existing schedules. GSA will, however, collect information on products that are on existing schedule to determine "which products are year-2000 compliant." Agencies can also use the definition of year-2000 compliance when they purchase software outside of GSA schedule.

In concert with efforts of the interagency committee, the National Institute of Standards and Technology (NIST) published a Federal Information Processing Standard on March 25, 1996, regarding Federal software purchases. The announcement (change no. 1 to FIPS 4-1) recommends that for purposes of electronic data interchange, federal agencies use four-digit year elements for data transmitted among US Government agencies. (See note 8) NIST chose not to require four-digit year elements for all interagency data transfer because it does not have authority to require federal agencies to comply. In addition, in many cases the four digit year field will not be necessary.

The interagency committee is involved with several other activities. On May 2, 1996, the committee cosponsored a conference bringing government and industry together to discuss year-2000 issues. The committee is currently developing a "best practice" report which will describe how agencies can best implement a solution. It will also include a comprehension conversion plan, setting milestones for Federal agency progress over the next few years. (See note 9) Through committee efforts, a site on the world wide web was developed to provide the latest information on year 2000 conversion activities. (See note 10) Private sector firms can also benefit from the information disseminated by the interagency committee.

Issues for Federal Agencies

Since there may not be enough time to complete year-2000 conversion for all information systems, federal agencies may have to prioritize their systems for repair. Several agencies are already admitting that there will likely be delays in other federal information technology projects due to the need to dedicate resources to year-2000 conversion. Non-critical computer systems may have to wait until after the start of year 2000. It is also possible that projects in areas other than information technology may have to be delayed or scaled back to divert funds to work on the year-2000 project. Funds may even have to be shifted from other agency accounts such, as research and development, procurement, operations, or maintenance. Individual agencies are confronting how they will prioritize their internal conversion projects. (See note 11)

The interagency committee recommends that Government agencies as well as private sector organizations conduct risk-benefit analyses before starting the conversion process. These analyses could help determine which systems absolutely must be fixed, and which could be terminated if their utility is not worth the effort needed to fix them. Unfortunately, the time taken to perform these analyses may delay the process of converting software. However, completing a risk analysis before starting the conversion is critical to help prioritize information technology systems.

Even a system that is year-2000 compliant can be contaminated by incorrect data entering from external interactions. Government agencies need to ensure that data entering their computer databases from other sources (such as state, county, municipal government, and the private sectors is accurate. To forestall contamination of federal databases, some suggest that OMB set a policy for how agencies monitor incoming data to insure its integrity. Many Federal agencies, however, would prefer to set their own rules for accepting external data.

STATUS OF STATE GOVERNMENTS, PRIVATE SECTOR, AND FOREIGN GOVERNMENT EFFORTS

Efforts needed to correct the problem in state and local government operations also are likely to be significant. The Gartner Group predicts that fewer than 25% of state and local government computer systems will be ready for the year 2000. The State of Nebraska estimates it will cost $28 million to pay for the conversion of its 12,000 computer programs and 12 million lines of code. Nebraska plans to divert part of its cigarette tax to provide $11.5 million toward conversion activities. Los Angeles county has made an initial estimate of $30 million for conversion costs, not including planning, testing, and unexpected hardware and software upgrades. (See note 12)

Major industry groups will need to make coordinated efforts to convert their software so that they can continue to interoperate as they do today. The securities industry, for example, must be able to perform stock transactions, access investor accounts, and record deposits and trades among business affiliates on a timely basis. For this to occur, all securities companies must agree on a standard year format for various types of data. Other industries that must coordinate their year 2000 efforts include banks, insurance companies, telecommunications providers, computer manufacturers, and airlines. In addition to fixing their own systems, many computer companies are beginning to market their services in year-2000 conversion.

Foreign companies and governments appear to be further behind in addressing the year-2000 than their counterparts in the United States. In May, 1996, the Chief Executive of the British Government Central Computer and Telecommunications Agency met with representatives of US Federal agencies and congressional staff to gain insights into dealing with the challenge. The science and technology attaches at the embassies of Canada, Japan, Germany, and Australia were unable to provide an assessment of the efforts taking place in their countries. There has been little press and government published assessments, indicating a lesser awareness of the issue in these countries than in the United States. (See note 13)

CONGRESSIONAL ACTIVITY

On April 16, 1996, the House Government Oversight and Reform Committee, Subcommittee on Government

Management, Information and Technology held a hearing to determine the extent of the problem, and how federal agencies are dealing with it. All witnesses stressed that federal government and other computer users must address this issue immediately. Following the hearing, the Subcommittee submitted a set of questions for major federal departments and agencies to determine their level of progress in addressing the issue. Information obtained from responses (due on June 7, 1996) will be analyzed by the General Accounting Office.

On May 14, 1996, the House Science Committee, Subcommittee on technology, held a hearing to review potential technical solutions to the year-2000 challenge, and to discuss a possible role for government in addressing the problem. Again, witnesses stressed the urgency needed to convert all software in a timely manner in both government and the private sector.

The FY1997 Senate Defense authorization bill (S. 1745) contained a provision directing DOD to assess the risk to its systems resulting from the year-2000 challenge, and to report to Congress on the resources necessary for conversion. The bill also require that all information technology purchased by DOD be able to operate in 2000 without modification, The bill was reported by the Senate Armed Services Committee on May 3, 1996;. Other congressional committees are interested in the year-2000 issue and may hold hearings to pursue their particular interest in the issue.

ISSUES AND OPTIONS FOR CONGRESS

Is the Problem Serious Enough to Warrant Congressional Action?

Many in Congress would prefer to let industry solve technical issues of this sort, allowing market forces to work and avoiding cost subsidies and counterproductive regulation, Others are concerned that this problem is so pervasive that it could affect the entire nation, including Federal, state, and local government, businesses, and personal activities, with potentially harmful consequences to the overall economy. Some in Congress have expressed an interest in using legislation to help reduce the negative effects of what may become a crisis situation. Some are concerned that media sensationalism of the problem could effect consumer confidence in institutions, such as banks, and in public institutions that provide services to citizens. Effective management by Federal officials and communication by policy makers could mitigate those effects.

What Are the Options for Congressional Action?

More funding. One option is to provide specific funding for federal information resources management (IRM) offices to convert their agency software. Some in federal agencies have voiced concerns that in order to maximize additional funding, IRM managers might delay conversion effort. Congress could, however, use a funding mechanism that matches funds dedicated by agencies to work on year-2000 conversion. This could have the effect of -stimulating agencies to put more resources on the problem. Finding new money, however, when Congress is focusing on reducing the Federal deficit will be a challenge. Some in federal agencies believe that funding could not realistically be provided until FY1998 appropriations, which will be too late for most agencies to begin work.

Reprogramming funds. The interagency committee advocates giving federal agencies greater autonomy in reprogramming funds to year-2000 efforts. Rules for reprogramming differ from agency to agency, and from year to year, however, depending on how each agency's appropriations legislation is written. Some appropriations subcommittees require approval before any funds are reprogrammed, while others allow various degrees of reprogramming among programs and accounts. Congress could create a special provision to allow agencies to reprogram for year-2000 efforts as part of a budget bill. If legislation to replace the process of reprogramming funds is passed this year, agencies could begin reprogramming in FY1997. Without general reprogramming authority for FY1997, agencies will have to wait another year to seek congressional approval, which may be too late to start year-2000 conversion.

At the April 16 hearing of the House Subcommittee on Government Management, Information and Technology, DOD expressed the need to be able to shift funds more quickly than the legislative process will allow in order to meet the year-2000 deadline. (See note 14) DOD has had problems obtaining timely approval for reprogramming funds for all of its programs. Currently, DOD can reprogram up to $10 million for procurement and up to $4 million for research and development in a given program without obtaining congressional approval. To reprogram funds in excess of these levels, DOD submits an omnibus reprogramming request each year containing dozens of requested funding changes. Only those items that receive the approval of all four defense budget oversight committees can be implemented.

DOD is now proposing legislation to allow it to double the amount of funds it can reprogram without congressional approval. DOD may also seek the authority to transfer funds between accounts (procurement to research and development, for instance) without congressional approval. (See note 15) While Congress may be reluctant to give DOD such a broad authority, a special limited provision might be considered for year 2000 efforts. Civilians agencies may want to gain similar authority for year-2000 efforts, although they have not requested it. Many agencies may not yet realize that they will need additional funds for year-2000 efforts.

Continued oversight. Others suggest that Congress take a different approach by continuing its oversight and scrutiny of federal efforts, and raising public awareness through hearings and written communication. While this may spur agencies into action, it would not help them to complete the work of software conversion. Congressional oversight can focus on how local agencies are prioritizing their computer systems projects, how money is being spent, and how potential delay could impact government operation. Further investigation into how state and local governments are preparing for year-2000 software conversion may be considered. The planned GAO study may provide information for Congress to take further action.

Standards issues. In the future, vendors might face potential liability for failure to provide year-2000 compliant products or services. Company managers may still need to be aware of whether their information suppliers are year-2000 compliant so that their databases are not corrupted by bad data. Businesses and government agencies may require software maintenance providers to accept contract provisions that require that computer systems continue to function properly after the year 2000. Banks, investment companies, and insurance companies may want to know whether companies they finance are year-2000 compliant before making some investment decisions.

These concerns raise questions about how consumer and government agencies can be sure that consultants and vendors are being honest about whether their products are year-2000 compliant. At the May 14 House Science Committee, Technology Subcommittee hearing, members raised questions as to whether the force of law is necessary to set standards for computer year fields. It was suggested that legislating a four digit year field standard for all electronic date interchange with the federal government would help bring the computer industry into compliance, and would at least raise awareness of the problem. Industry witnesses testified that if standards are necessary, they should be developed under the auspices of the American National Standards Institute (ANSI), a private sector, voluntary, consensus standards setting organization for the computer and electronics industry, rather than dictated by Congress. Other members warned that legislating standards was unnecessary and might not even contribute to raising public awareness. Notably, by the time an industry consensus standard is worked out, it might be too late.

International issues. Because the United States is more heavily dependent on computers than other nations, the year-2000 is probably a greater challenge here than anywhere else. The economic impacts of business failing to correct the problem, both domestically and internationally, could be dramatic. US businesses and government agencies will probably lead the rest of the world in fostering awareness and in assisting in software conversion. DOD is currently discussing with the NATO allies the need to ensure their year-2000 computer capability for future military engagements or other collaborative operations, and the general sharing of data. This area may require increased attention. The State Department may need to become involved in spreading awareness of this issue internationally through the diplomatic corps at US embassies in foreign countries. US. federal agencies and businesses may need to emphasize the urgency of correcting the problem in making international agreements. Congressional attention to this issue helps to increase awareness in other countries.

The future. This issue's sudden rise to public attention leads to the question of whether we can identify and prevent comparable technology problems before they reach these proportions. the computer industry has managed to deal with other problems reasonably well without federal intervention. Viruses, for example, became a widespread problem starting in the late 1980's. In response, anti-virus software was developed commercially and became widely used. Now, it is considered standard procedure for all data entering a computer to be checked first for viruses. Various security features are also now available and can be added to computing systems as threats are presented. Perhaps other unforeseen software upgrades will be necessary for widespread computer applications. As other computer-related issues continue to arise, Congress may again be faced with deciding what role the federal government should play in ensuring security and reliability in federal computer systems, and providing guidance and leadership into the digital age.

Notes:

1. It is assumed that the Mitre Corp. has no incentive to exaggerate, because its funding is limited by Congress and working on year-2000 projects would preclude it from working on other projects. Another independent source (Peter DeJager, private consultant) places the Gartner Group estimate at the low end of the range of possible costs.

2. Nickolas Zvegintsov, the Year 2000 as Racket and Ruse. American Programmer, Feb. 1966.

3. Bruce Hall, Research Director, Applications Management Division, Gartner Group, Federal Conference on

Year 2000 Conversion, Dept. of Commerce, May 2, 1996.

4. Before hiring a contractor, some organizations have checked the validity of the contractor's assessment of the problem by running an independent software analyzer on their software code.

5. Testimony of D. Dean. Mesterharm, Deputy commissioner for Systems, social security Administration, before the House Subcommittee on Government Management, Information and Technology, April 16, 1996.

6. Testimony of Emmett Paige, Jr., Assistant Secretary of Defense (C3I) before the House subcommittee on Government Management, Information and Technology, April 6, 1996.

7. Last year Treasury collected $1.4 trillion and processed over 250 million returns. The treasury Financial Management Services oversees a daily cash flow in excess of $10 billion and issues 800 million payments totaling over $1 trillion each year for all executive agencies. The Customs Service collects over $20 billion annually in duties, taxes and fees.   Public debt auctions $2 trillion marketable Treasury securities annually, issues and redeems 150 million savings bonds annually, and accounts for $4.9 trillion federal debt and over $300 billion in annual interest charges. All of these critical activities use computer support that must be inspected and corrected for year-2000 compliance.

8. Private industry currently uses a two-digit year standard for data interchange.

9. The best practices document offers a method for dividing year-2000 conversion activities into five phases: awareness, assessment, renovation, validation and implementation. The document should be available on the world wide web by mid July (Information obtained from minutes of interagency committee meeting of May 8, 1966.

10. The address of the web page, managed by GSA, is http://www/itpolicy/library/yr2000/y201tocl.htm. The web page is hyper-linked to DOD and other Federal agency year-2000 web pages. Numerous other World Wide Web pages are maintained by government and private sector organizations discussing activities and available resources on year-2000 conversion.

11. Information systems managers in the House, Senate and Library of Congress are working on the year-2000 for their systems, and expect to be compliant well before the end of the century.

12. "The Clock is Ticking: Year 2000 Does Not Compute", County News, National Assn. of Counties, April 29, 1996.

13. Personal telephone conversations with foreign attaches, March-April, 1996.

14. Testimony of Emmett Paige, Jr. before the House Subcommittee on Government Management, Information and Technology, April 16, 1996.

15. "Pentagon to Propose Thresholds for Reprogramming", Inside the Pentagon, May 23, 1996.

"I'm taking the time for a number of things
That weren't important yesterday."

"Fixing a Hole" - the Beatles

Appendix D

Emergency Preparedness Vendor Directory

Six times a year, the publishers of the news magazine, The Preparedness Journal, (801-265-8828) conduct Preparedness Expos around the United States. The following directory provides a listing of some of the the exhibitors at the 1996 shows. They offer food, water, and other commodity storage goods, books and other publications and preparedness equipment. I do not endorse any of these vendors (unless specifically noted) and I have no relationship of any kind with any of them. I provide this listing solely as a service to my readers.

Alco-Bright Co, Inc.
Post Office Box 840926
Hildale, Utah 84784
(801) 874-1025

"Emergency Heat" indoor-outdoor gelled ethanol fuel and dampered "Snap-On-Stove". Keep Warm, boil water, cook food, provide light in your home, car, tent or shelter. Steel cans provide long storage life for 72 hr. emergency kits.

Alpineaire Foods
Post Office Box 926
Nevada City, Nevada 95959
(800) 322-6325

Quality Shelf Stable foods which have a long storage life, and are free of artificial additives. Established in 1975, we specialize in foods which require no cooking - just add water. Over 200 items available in cans and pouches. Also carry full line of backpacking meals.

American Brain Storm Innovation
Post Office 141
75 South Main
Glendale, Utah 84729
(800) 505-0514

The perfect tool for all your gardening needs! Extend your growing season with an Environmental Enclosure Systems Greenhouse. Steel construction, high wind resistance, Low Cost ! Protect your harvest from weeds, Insects and weather!

Approved First Aid, Inc..
Post Office Box 8010
Fort Worth, Texas 76124
(817) 654-2234 (800) 472-8419

Complete Line of First Aid Supplies. We offer sales and service of first aid kits and safety equipment. We also carry a full line of K.T. Medical, Power lift back saver, wrist braces, ankle braces, elbow braces, knee braces.

Aspects of Self-reliance
1330 Mill Holland Ave.
Clermont, Florida 34711
(407) 574-5439

Emergency Water Storage featuring Softank foldable, durable, reusable pillow tank constructed with a tough cross-laminated FDA approval material. Sizes 30 to 200 gallons. Easily stored until ready for use. Solid water tanks available also.

Christian Family Resources
Post Office Box 195
Kit Carson, Colorado 80825
(719) 962-3228

Your one stop supplier for: Grain Mills, Bread Making Equipment and Supplies, Dehydrated Food Storage, Non-electric Tools and Appliances, Personal and Home Protection, Extreme Pressure Lubricant, Home Schooling Material. Catalog $1.00. Store Hours Mon.-Sat. 1:00 pm to 6:00pm MST.

Country Harvest Foods
325 West 600 South
Heber City, Utah 84032
Orders:(800) 322-2245/(801) 654-5400

"Someone is finally doing food storage right!" We have
the most modern canning facility in the business. 99.9%
oxygen free and nitrogen packed. We carry a full line of
the best dehydrated foods available on the market today.
We also carry the best 72-hour kits, first-aid kits and everything for your preparedness needs.

Country Living Products
14727 56th Avenue NW
Stanwood, Washington 98292
(206) 652-0671

With or without electricity, C.L. Mill outgrinds them all.
Industrial bearings, balanced browning flywheel. Many-
lifetimes-rugged. Built smart for tough times. 20 year war-
ranty. "Country Living Mill" designed for those with
vision beyond today!

Countryside & Small Stock Journal
W 11564-P Hwy. 64
Withee, Wisconsin 54498
(800) 551-5691

Be self-reliant through simple country living. Garden,
raise livestock, preserve food, provide basics, much more.
Be prepared, and enjoy life! Learn from those doing it.
Our 78th year.

Emergency Essentials
National Catalog Sales Office
165 S. Mountain Way Drive
Orem, Utah 84058
(801) 222-9596 (800) 999-1863 Toll Free Order Line

We have the most complete selection of preparedness supplies for your car, home, school and office. 72-Hour Kits, First Aid Kits, Food Storage, MRE's, Water Purifiers and Storage Containers and much more are available through our color catalogs and newsletters. Call us today, and we'll help you "be prepared" at the lowest prices available -- guaranteed.

EVP Enterprises
Post Office Box 74
Rigby, Idaho 83442

Save $$ hundreds. Dry your own survival foods at home. Time-tested 30-page manual with diagrams and instructions for building inexpensive dryers, and directions for drying, curing and storing fruits, vegetables and meat. $10.00 post paid, check or M.O.

Family Preparedness Handbook
by James T. Stevens
15123 Little Wren Lane
San Antonio, Texas 78255
(210) 695-5108

Family Preparedness Handbook, new & revised 8th Edition. More than 500 pages of information about family preparedness and food storage. 100s of listings for what and where to buy food storage items! 100s of recipes. More than 300,000 copies sold.

(Note: In the Survival Guide, I have heartily endorsed this excellent book. JML)

Future Foods
Post Office Box 1922
Orem, Utah 84059-1922
(800) 949-FOOD (3663)

Buy a years supply of groceries in advance for no money down and 0% interest for an entire year. Finally, pantry size cans that are packaged for both long term storage, convenience and every day use. Award winning foods voted best tasting by consumers. Enjoy foods like Aunt Pearls Soups and Sauces, NutriFruit Jells, puddings, apple cinnamon pancakes, scones, muffins, fruit, vegetables, passionate peach drink, an entire line of UN-Meat products, creamy mashed potatoes and gravy, real milk you stir with a spoon, nutritional drinks, Fat Free   cookie mixes (Double Chocolate Fudge) etc. Nothing like it in the industry! Our foods are sold in grocery stores and used in restaurants and are only the highest quality to meet consumer demands.O% Interest financing available on approved credit, No Money Down, Pay as little as $50 per month for an entire year supply. No shipping charges on multiple units purchased. Receive entire order within 14 days of credit approval and make no payments for 30 days. Call Toll Free: 1-800-949-FOOD (3663)

Homestead Foods
Post Office Box 96
Victor, Montana 59875
(800) 838-3132

Specializing in Alpineaire Gourmet Reserves, the finest all-natural, shelf-stable food storage systems available.

Best tasting, large portions, convenient (just add water). Cans or back-pack pouches. Demanding situations call for top energy and health. Don't settle for less.

Major Surplus
435 W. Alondra Boulevard
Gardena, California 90248
(800) 441-8855

The Leader in Disaster Preparedness. A complete line of products & kits for home, office, school and tra٧ ٤l. Call for FREE catalog and customized preparedness pla.٦. Whole-sale and Group pricing available.

Magic Mill
3686 South 2455 East
Salt Lake City, Utah 84109
(801) 943-8860

Mill, Mixer, Slicer, Dehydrator, Automatic Bread Maker, Sun Oven, Foodsaver Juicers & Hand Mill, along with sprouts & seeds, grains, wheat, baking aids: yeast dough enhancer, gluten, flour, food storage items, seasoning, cleaning products and health & care products.

Marlene's Magic
4958 Alpine Circle
Highland, Utah 84003
(801) 756-6423

Our latest book-Marlene's Magic with Food Storage - takes you through seven steps of purchasing and organizing your food storage inexpensively with nutrition in mind. Over 500 Recipes. Marlene's 40-years of training in food preparation gives you delicious and nutritious meals that children, teenagers and adults will eat.

Nitro-Pak Preparedness Center
147 No. Main Street
Heber City, Utah 84302
(800) 866-4876

America's #1 source for survival supplies and foods. NI-TRO-PAK is well-known for their premium quality dehydrated and freeze-dried "no-cook" storage foods. They also offer a full line of 72-hour emergency kits, year supply units, 1st aid kits, water storage containers and filters, military ready-to-eat meals (MRE's), wheat and grain mills, personal protection devices, preparedness books and videos and much more. Call or write for their complete catalog—just $3.

Optimum Energy
Preparedness Center for Home, Camp & Emergency
106 Yelm Avenue West
Post Office Box 1979
Yelm, Washington 98597
(360) 458-4602 Fax (360) 458-9102

The most comprehensive selection of power outage supplies and emergency preparedness items in the Pacific Northwest. We have a full line of Ready-to-go emergency supply kits for family, workplace and vehicle. Plus, we carry evacuation & camping supplies and everything youd need to sustain yourself at home for an extended period of time with no power or water. Emergency kits, portable water filters, plastic water barrels, dehydrated food, portable stoves, hand crank/solar radios, kitchen supplies, books, day packs & backpacks, tents, sleeping bags, camping gear, sanitation supplies, tools alternative lighting, first aid, hand pumps for wells and much more. Catalog available for $3 or visit our store in downtown Yelm,

WA. We accept MC, VISA and Discover.

Preparedness Resources
3999 South Main, Suite S-2
Salt Lake City, Utah 84107
(801) 268-3913, ext. 125

Perma Pak has been the leader in the food storage business for over 40 years. We carry a full line of dehydrated foods as well as 72-hour Emergency Kits and other items for Emergency Preparedness.

Ponderosa Sports & Mercantile, Inc.
Post Office Box 1016
Eagle, Idaho 83616
(208) 939-1513

Ponderosa Products is a mom and pop company specializing in preparedness food, equipment and supplies. We offer MRE's, freeze dried foods, Heatermeals, BFM (Balanced Food Mix), first aid kits & supplies, guns, ammunition, magazines, pepper sprays, knives, kevlar vests, military surplus, survival manuals & supplies, llama pack equipment, chemlights, and more. for our 26 page catalog, send $1.

Rainy Day Foods
Post Office Box 1901
Cedar Town, Georgia 30125
(770) 748-3297

Rainy Day Supply can help you be prepared for almost any emergency, on the road or at home. Come see our line of "Sam Andy," low moisture foods and our ideas for storing grains. Also other great items for total preparation.

Ready Reserve Foods
Post Office Box 697
Beaumont, California 92223
(800) 453-2202

A full line of Emergency Preparedness items including over 100 different dry food products for long term storage.

Rodnoy Corporation
13231 Brainwood Ave.
Warren, Michigan 48089
(810) 758-7132

NEW TECHNOLOGY. Worlds greatest, longest lasting hand held flashlight. Hurricanes, earthquakes, blizzards. Small, lightweight, durable, 8+ year shelf life. Never be in the dark again. Runs 2800+ Hours on 2 D-cells. $9.95. FREE RECORDED MESSAGE. (800) 710-09121

Product Concepts Company
Post Office Box 596
Hayesville, North Carolina 28904
(704) 389-3301

The FloGo line of purification products are the most effective and cost saving products ever available. The FloGl bottle is a patented sub micron filtration bottle which produces 200 gallons of pure, clean water for only $19.95. Pure Water, anywhere...anytime.

Sam Andy Foods
800 West Airport Frwy., Ste. #1100
Irving, Texas 75062
(214) 445-4144 (800) 331-0358

The oldest and biggest company in the industry with the

largest line of products. Sam Andy is world-famous for its low-moisture, long-life food products, equipment, supplies and information for survival and emergency preparedness. We publish a periodic newsletter - call us to request your FREE copy! Dealer opportunities available.

Star Food Processing Inc..
3444 East Commerce Street
San Antonio, Texas 78220
(800) 882-MEAL

Fully cooked Heat & Eat serving trays. Entrees Include: Campfire Stew, Chili Cookoff, Chuckwagon Chicken, The Whole Enchilada, Spaghetti Western, Sunday Chicken & Texas Grub Steak. Each tray contains 106 ounces of fully cooked, ready to eat products. Thirty minutes is the time required to prepare a delicious meal from pantry to the table. This product is shelf stable and requires no refrigeration or freezing for storage. Normal shelf life is two years.

Storehouse Products
Post Office Box 690021
San Antonio Texas 78269
(210) 690-7632

A Texas distributor providing a complete line of dehydrated foods, grain mills, water purification systems, 72-hour kits, and many other emergency preparedness items. Call or write for a FREE catalogue.

Survival Associates, Inc..
Post Office Box 6426
Titusville, Florida 32782
(407) 269-6059

Emergency survival food, weight 1 lb. food for 1 person for 15 days 10 years shelf life.

The Cookbook Shoppe
Vickie Tate
302 East 200 North
Manti, Utah 84642
(801) 835-8283

A collection of the best Home Storage & Preparedness Books including the best selling Cooking With Home Storage.

The Preparedness Store
Post Office Box 211503
Bedford, Texas 76095
(817) 354-8946

Serving TEXAS from the DFW area with Disaster Preparedness Supplies, Food and Water Storage, First Aid Kits, and Home/Office/Travel Emergency Kits. Your Local Supplier for Preparedness Products.

The Survival Center
19223 Cook Road, Box 234
McKenna, Washington 98558
(206) 458-6778

600+ Item Catalog of Health & Survival Products. Food Storage, Wilderness Supplies, Water Purification, Underground Shelters & Equipment, Food Preservation, Food Preparation, Sanitation Equipment, Emergency Protection Supplies, Homesteading Supplies, Hunting Equipment, Water Storage, Books, Herbs & More. For our catalog send $2.00 to The Survival Center.

To Order This Book or Jim Lord's

Year 2000 Survival Newsletter

Call (Toll Free)

1-888-Y2K-2555

A Survival Guide For The Year 2000 Problem	$29.97
Jim Lord's Year 2000 Survival Newsletter (1 Year)	$129.00
Book plus Newsletter (1 Year)	$119.00
Book plus Newsletter (3 Years)	$229.00

(Maryland residents add 5% sales tax)

* * Please add $5 shipping & handling for each book ordered * *
(All orders are sent via Priority Mail)

<u>Volume discounts available. Please inquire.</u>

Publisher's Management Corp.   Internet: WWW.SurviveY2K.com
2320 W. Peoria Ave., #C122
Phoenix AZ 85029-4767

Guarantee

The above products are offered with a 100% risk-free guarantee of satisfaction. If you are unsatisfied for any reason at all, you can return the product within 45 days of purchase for a prompt refund.